Granny's Favourites

This edition published in 2010

LOVE FOOD is an imprint of Parragon Books Ltd

Parragon
Queen Street House
4 Queen Street
Bath BA1 1HE, UK

Copyright © Parragon Books Ltd 2010

LOVE FOOD and the accompanying heart device is a registered trade mark of Parragon Books Ltd in Australia, the UK, USA, India and the EU.

ISBN: 978-1-4454-2233-6

Printed in China

Notes for the Reader
This book uses both metric and imperial measurements. Follow the same units of measurement throughout; do not mix metric and imperial. All spoon measurements are level: teaspoons are assumed to be 5 ml, and tablespoons are assumed to be 15 ml. Unless otherwise stated, milk is assumed to be full fat, eggs and individual vegetables are medium, and pepper is freshly ground black pepper.

The times given are an approximate guide only. Preparation times differ according to the techniques used by different people and the cooking times may also vary from those given. Optional ingredients, variations or serving suggestions have not been included in the calculations.

Recipes using raw or very lightly cooked eggs should be avoided by infants, the elderly, pregnant women, convalescents and anyone suffering from an illness. Pregnant and breastfeeding women are advised to avoid eating peanuts and peanut products. Sufferers from nut allergies should be aware that some of the ready-made ingredients used in the recipes in this book may contain nuts. Always check the packaging before use.

Granny's Favourites

introduction

For many of us, our childhoods were very much linked to our grandparents. When we visited them for Christmas and other holidays, all the traditional foods would appear as if by magic. It is only with hindsight that we appreciate the amount of planning and hard work that went into making our perfect holidays. Often we would not only be able to eat the food but also have the thrill of helping to make it. Somehow, Granny always had time to allow us to roll out the pastry and biscuits and help mix the cakes. She even allowed us to lick the delicious mix before it went in the oven. It was here that many of us learned to cook as Granny was able to spend time with us and pass on the considerable knowledge that she had acquired over the years.

Today's generation of grandmothers is more likely to be engaged full-time in the workplace and trying to juggle home, family, work, hobbies, interests and travels abroad. Her time for cooking has been reduced and she probably saves the traditional foods for special occasions and chooses quicker and healthier recipes in her day-to-day cooking. Her food habits are changing too, influenced by travel to far-away places and sampling the local fare. We also have a wider variety of food ingredients available, making many exciting new recipes and exotic meals far more accessible.

As the years have passed, our eating habits have changed. Foods that would have been considered exotic twenty years ago have become part of our everyday life. Chicken tikka masala has overtaken roast beef as our nation's favourite dish. Pizza is another example of a food which has been absorbed into our national food identity along with others, such as chicken kiev, spaghetti bolognese and chilli con carne. This is a result of the changing population

of our own country and the fact that many of us now have the opportunity to travel throughout the world. Most of our grandparents did not get the chance to journey much further than their own backyards, but global travel has widened the range of food experiences for today's generation. South American, Asian and Eastern European foods have all become part of our regular diet in recent years.

Granny's
comfort food

Comfort foods are the old favourites: the meals that are particularly familiar to us, give us a warm feeling and soothe our souls. Granny made these for us when we were young, so the good feelings associated with them are still there. When we are upset, worried or depressed, simple food like a warming chicken or tomato soup is just what is needed.

Dishes that you can eat with your hands, such as a grilled cheese sandwich or a tasty hamburger, are just the thing when you don't feel like sitting at the table with a knife and fork. A casserole is an excellent standby for a cold winter's day and provides a great opportunity to get the family sitting around the table, eating and discussing the day's occurrences. Other familiar foods, like traditional roast chicken, fish pie and baked potatoes, are all covered in this chapter so, whenever you need them, you'll have heartening recipes to hand, just like the ones your Granny might have cooked for you.

tomato soup

ingredients

SERVES 4

55 g/2 oz butter

1 onion, finely chopped

700 g/1 lb 9 oz tomatoes,
    finely chopped

600 ml/1 pint hot chicken or
    vegetable stock

pinch of sugar

2 tbsp shredded fresh basil
    leaves, plus extra sprigs
    to garnish

1 tbsp chopped fresh parsley

salt and pepper

croûtons, to serve (optional)

method

1 Melt half the butter in a large, heavy-based saucepan. Add the onion and cook over a low heat, stirring occasionally, for 5 minutes, or until softened. Add the tomatoes, season to taste with salt and pepper and cook for 5 minutes.

2 Pour in the hot chicken or vegetable stock, return to the boil, then reduce the heat and cook for 10 minutes.

3 Push the soup through a sieve with the back of a wooden spoon to remove the tomato skins and seeds. Return to the saucepan and stir in the sugar, remaining butter, basil and parsley. Heat through briefly, but do not allow to boil. Ladle into warmed serving bowls. Serve immediately, garnished with sprigs of basil and accompanied by croûtons, if you wish.

cream of chicken soup

ingredients

SERVES 4

3 tbsp butter

4 shallots, chopped

1 leek, trimmed and sliced

450 g/1 lb skinless chicken
    breasts, chopped

600 ml/1 pint chicken stock

1 tbsp chopped fresh parsley

1 tbsp chopped fresh thyme

175 ml/6 fl oz double cream

salt and pepper

sprigs of fresh thyme,
    to garnish

fresh crusty rolls, to serve

method

1 Melt the butter in a large saucepan over a medium heat. Add the shallots and cook, stirring, for 3 minutes, until slightly softened. Add the leek and cook for a further 5 minutes, stirring. Add the chicken, stock and herbs, and season with salt and pepper. Bring to the boil, then lower the heat and simmer for 25 minutes, until the chicken is tender and cooked through. Remove from the heat and leave to cool for 10 minutes.

2 Transfer the soup into a food processor and blend until smooth (you may need to do this in batches). Return the soup to the pan and warm over a low heat for 5 minutes.

3 Stir in the cream and cook for a further 2 minutes, then remove from the heat and ladle into serving bowls. Garnish with sprigs of thyme and serve with fresh crusty rolls.

grilled cheese sandwich

ingredients

SERVES 2

100 g/3^1/$_2$ oz Gruyère or
    Emmental cheese, grated
4 slices white bread, with the
    crusts trimmed
2 thick slices ham
1 small egg, beaten
150 ml/5 fl oz shop-bought
    white sauce
3 tbsp unsalted butter,
    plus extra if necessary

method

1 Spread half the cheese on 2 bread slices, then top each with a slice of ham, cut to fit. Sprinkle the ham with all but 2 tablespoons of the remaining cheese, then sandwich together with the remaining bread slices and press down well.

2 Beat the egg in a shallow dish. Add 1 sandwich and press down to coat on both sides, then remove from the dish and repeat with the other sandwich. Meanwhile, gently heat the sauce. Keep warm.

3 Preheat the grill to high. Line a baking tray with foil and set aside. Melt the butter in a sauté pan or frying pan and cook 1 or both sandwiches, depending on the size of your pan, over a medium-high heat until golden brown on both sides. Add a little extra butter, if necessary, if you have to cook the sandwiches separately.

4 Transfer the sandwiches to the foil-lined baking tray and spread the white sauce over the top. Cook under the grill, about 10 cm/ 4 inches from the heat, for 4 minutes, or until golden and brown.

roast chicken

ingredients

SERVES 6

1 free-range chicken,
  weighing 2.25 kg/5 lb
55 g/2 oz butter
2 tbsp chopped fresh lemon
  thyme
1 lemon, quartered
125 ml/4 fl oz white wine
salt and pepper
6 fresh thyme sprigs,
  to garnish

method

1 Preheat the oven to 220°C/425°F/Gas Mark 7 and place the chicken in a roasting tin.

2 Place the butter in a bowl and soften with a fork, then mix in the thyme and season well with salt and pepper. Butter the chicken all over with the herb butter, inside and out, and place the lemon quarters inside the body cavity. Pour the wine over the chicken.

3 Roast the chicken in the centre of the oven for 20 minutes. Reduce the temperature to 190°C/375°F/Gas Mark 5 and continue to roast for a further 1$1/4$ hours, basting frequently. Cover with foil if the skin begins to brown too much. If the tin dries out, add a little more wine or water.

4 Test that the chicken is cooked by piercing the thickest part of the leg with a sharp knife or skewer and making sure the juices run clear. Remove from the oven.

5 Remove the chicken from the roasting tin and place on a warmed serving plate to rest, covered with foil, for 10 minutes before carving.

6 Place the roasting tin on the top of the hob and bubble the pan juices gently over a low heat until they have reduced and are thick and glossy. Season to taste.

7 Serve the chicken with the pan juices and scatter with the thyme sprigs.

potato, leek & chicken pie

ingredients

SERVES 4

225 g/8 oz waxy potatoes,
    cubed

5 tbsp butter

1 skinless chicken breast
    fillet, about 175 g/6 oz,
    cubed

1 leek, sliced

150 g/5^1/$_2$ oz chestnut
    mushrooms, sliced

2^1/$_2$ tbsp plain flour

300 ml/10 fl oz milk

1 tbsp Dijon mustard

2 tbsp chopped fresh sage

225 g/8 oz filo pastry, thawed
    if frozen

3 tbsp butter, melted

salt and pepper

method

1 Preheat the oven to 180°C/350°F/
Gas Mark 4. Cook the potato cubes in a
saucepan of boiling water for 5 minutes.
Drain and set aside.

2 Melt the butter in a frying pan and cook the
chicken cubes for 5 minutes or until browned
all over.

3 Add the leek and mushrooms and cook for
3 minutes, stirring. Stir in the flour and cook
for 1 minute stirring constantly. Gradually
stir in the milk and bring to the boil. Add the
mustard, sage and potato cubes, season to
taste with salt and pepper and simmer for
10 minutes.

4 Meanwhile, line a deep pie dish with half
of the sheets of filo pastry. Spoon the sauce
into the dish and cover with 1 sheet of pastry.
Brush the pastry with butter and lay another
sheet on top. Brush this sheet with butter.

5 Cut the remaining filo pastry into strips and
fold them on to the top of the pie to create a
ruffled effect. Brush the strips with the melted
butter and cook in the preheated oven for
45 minutes or until golden brown and crisp.
Serve hot.

roast beef

ingredients

SERVES 8

1 prime rib of beef joint,
  weighing 2.7 kg/6 lb
2 tsp dry English mustard
3 tbsp plain flour
300 ml/10 fl oz red wine
300 ml/10 fl oz beef stock
salt and pepper
Yorkshire puddings, to serve

method

1 Preheat the oven to 230°C/450°F/ Gas Mark 8.

2 Season the meat to taste with salt and pepper. Rub in the mustard and 1 tablespoon of the flour.

3 Place the meat in a roasting tin and roast in the oven for 15 minutes. Reduce the temperature to 190°C/375°F/Gas Mark 5 and cook for 15 minutes per 450 g/1 lb, plus 15 minutes (1^3/4 hours for this joint) for rare beef or 20 minutes per 450 g/1 lb, plus 20 minutes (2 hours 20 minutes) for medium beef. Baste the meat from time to time to keep it moist.

4 Remove the meat from the oven, cover with foil and leave in a warm place for 10–15 minutes.

5 To make the gravy, pour off most of the fat from the tin, leaving behind the meat juices and the sediment. Place the tin on the hob over a medium heat and scrape all the sediment from the base of the tin. Sprinkle in the remaining flour and quickly whisk it into the juices. When you have a smooth paste, gradually add the wine and most of the stock, whisking constantly. Bring to the boil, then reduce the heat to a gentle simmer and cook for 2–3 minutes. Season and add the remaining stock.

6 Carve the meat, and serve with the gravy and Yorkshire puddings.

beef in beer with herb dumplings

ingredients

SERVES 6

2 tbsp sunflower oil

2 large onions, thinly sliced

8 carrots, sliced

4 tbsp plain flour

1.25 kg/2 lb 12 oz stewing
  steak, cut into cubes

425 ml/15 fl oz stout

2 tsp muscovado sugar

2 bay leaves

1 tbsp chopped fresh thyme

salt and pepper

for the herb dumplings

115 g/4 oz self-raising flour

pinch of salt

55 g/2 oz shredded suet

2 tbsp chopped fresh parsley,
  plus extra to garnish

about 4 tbsp water

method

1 Preheat the oven to 160°C/325°F/Gas Mark 3. Heat the oil in a flameproof casserole. Add the onions and carrots and cook over a low heat, stirring occasionally, for 5 minutes, or until the onions are softened. Meanwhile, place the flour in a polythene bag and season with salt and pepper. Add the stewing steak to the bag, tie the top and shake well to coat. Do this in batches, if necessary.

2 Remove the vegetables from the casserole with a slotted spoon and reserve. Add the stewing steak to the casserole, in batches, and cook, stirring frequently, until browned all over. Return all the meat and the onions and carrots to the casserole and sprinkle in any remaining seasoned flour. Pour in the stout and add the sugar, bay leaves and thyme. Bring to the boil, cover and transfer to the preheated oven to bake for 1 3/4 hours.

3 To make the herb dumplings, sift the flour and salt into a bowl. Stir in the suet and parsley and add enough of the water to make a soft dough. Shape into small balls between the palms of your hands. Add to the casserole and return to the oven for 30 minutes. Remove and discard the bay leaves. Serve immediately, sprinkled with chopped parsley.

steak & kidney pie

ingredients

SERVES 4–6

900 g/2 lb stewing steak,
   trimmed of excess fat and
   cut into 2.5-cm/1-inch
   cubes
225 g/8 oz lamb's kidneys,
   cored and diced
2 tbsp plain flour
2 tsp dried mixed herbs
55 g/2 oz butter
1 onion, thinly sliced
300 ml/10 fl oz beef stock
1 tbsp Worcestershire sauce
salt and pepper

pastry

175 g/6 oz plain flour, plus
   extra for dusting
140 g/5 oz butter, diced
about 3 tbsp iced water
1 egg, lightly beaten
salt

method

1 Mix together the steak, kidneys, flour and herbs and season. Melt half the butter in a large pan. Cook the onion over a low heat for 5 minutes. Add the remaining butter and the meat mixture. Increase the heat and cook, stirring frequently, for 10 minutes. Pour in the stock and Worcestershire sauce and season. Bring to the boil, reduce the heat, cover and simmer, stirring occasionally, for $1^{1}/_{2}$–2 hours, until tender. Transfer to a large pie dish and leave to cool.

2 Meanwhile, make the pastry. Sift the flour with a pinch of salt into a bowl and add the butter and water. Mix to a firm but slightly lumpy dough. Roll out into a rectangle on a floured surface, then fold the top third down and the bottom third up. Give the dough a quarter turn, roll out and fold again. Repeat once more, then wrap and chill.

3 Preheat the oven to 230°C/450°F/Gas Mark 8. Roll out the pastry on a floured surface to 2.5 cm/1 inch larger than the top of the dish. Cut out a 15-mm/$^{5}/_{8}$-inch strip all the way around. Brush the rim of the dish with water and press the strip on to it. Brush with water and lift the remaining dough on top. Trim off the excess and crimp the edges to seal. Make a slit in the centre and brush with beaten egg. Roll out the trimmings and use to decorate the pie, then brush with beaten egg.

4. Bake for 10 minutes, then brush the pie with the remaining beaten egg. Reduce the oven temperature to 180°C/350°F/Gas Mark 4 and bake for a further 20 minutes, until the pastry is golden brown. Serve immediately.

hamburgers

ingredients

SERVES 4–6

450 g/1 lb rump steak or
  topside, freshly minced

1 onion, grated

2–4 garlic cloves, crushed

2 tsp wholegrain mustard

pepper

2 tbsp olive oil

450 g/1 lb onions, finely
  sliced

2 tsp light muscovado sugar

to serve

4–6 sesame seed buns

lettuce

ketchup (optional)

method

1 Place the minced steak, grated onion, garlic, mustard and pepper in a large bowl and mix together. Shape into 4–6 equal-sized burgers, then cover and leave to chill for 30 minutes.

2 Meanwhile, heat the oil in a heavy-based frying pan. Add the onions and cook over a low heat for 10–15 minutes, or until the onions have caramelized. Add the sugar after 8 minutes and stir occasionally during cooking. Drain well on kitchen paper and keep warm.

3 Wipe the frying pan clean, then heat until hot. When hot, add the burgers and cook for 3–5 minutes on each side or until cooked to personal preference. Serve in sesame seed buns with the onions, lettuce and ketchup, if you like.

shepherd's pie

ingredients

SERVES 6

1 tbsp olive oil

2 onions, finely chopped

2 garlic cloves, finely chopped

675 g/1 lb 8 oz good-quality
   lamb mince

2 carrots, finely chopped

1 tbsp plain flour

225 ml/8 fl oz beef or chicken
   stock

125 ml/4 fl oz red wine

salt and pepper

mashed potato

675 g/1 lb 8 oz floury
   potatoes, such as King
   Edward, Maris Piper or
   Desiree, peeled and cut
   into even-sized chunks

55 g/2 oz butter

2 tbsp cream or milk

method

1 Preheat the oven to 180°C/350°F/Gas Mark 4. Heat the oil in a large, flameproof casserole dish and fry the onion until softened, then add the garlic and stir well.

2 Raise the heat and add the meat. Cook quickly to brown the meat all over, stirring constantly. Add the carrots and season well with salt and pepper. Stir in the flour and add the stock and wine. Stir well and heat until simmering and thickened.

3 Cover the casserole dish and cook in the oven for about 1 hour. Check the consistency from time to time and add a little more stock or wine if required. The meat mixture should be quite thick but not dry. Season with salt and pepper.

4 While the meat is cooking, make the mashed potato. Cook the potatoes in a large saucepan of boiling salted water for 15–20 minutes. Drain well and mash with a potato masher until smooth. Add the butter and cream and season well with salt and pepper.

5 Spoon the lamb mixture into an ovenproof serving dish and spread or pipe the potato on top.

6 Increase the oven temperature to 200°C/400°F/Gas Mark 6 and cook the pie for 15–20 minutes at the top of the oven until golden brown.

toad in the hole

ingredients

SERVES 4

oil, for greasing

115 g/4 oz plain flour

pinch of salt

1 egg, beaten

300 ml/10 fl oz milk

450 g/1 lb good-quality pork
    sausages

1 tbsp vegetable oil

method

1 Grease a 20 x 25-cm/8 x 10-inch ovenproof dish or roasting tin.

2 Make the batter by sifting the flour and salt into a mixing bowl. Make a well in the centre and add the beaten egg and half the milk. Carefully stir the liquid into the flour until the mixture is smooth. Gradually beat in the remaining milk. Leave to stand for 30 minutes.

3 Preheat the oven to 220°C/425°F/ Gas Mark 7.

4 Prick the sausages and place them in the dish. Sprinkle over the oil and cook the sausages in the oven for 10 minutes until they are beginning to colour and the fat has started to run and is sizzling.

5 Remove from the oven and quickly pour the batter over the sausages. Return to the oven and cook for 35–45 minutes until the batter is well risen and golden brown. Serve immediately.

fish & chips

ingredients

SERVES 2

vegetable oil, for deep-frying

3 large potatoes, such as
　Cara or Desiree

2 thick cod or haddock fillets,
　175 g/6 oz each

175 g/6 oz self-raising flour,
　plus extra for dusting

200 ml/7 fl oz cold lager

salt and pepper

lemon wedges, to serve

method

1 Heat the oil in a temperature-controlled deep-fat fryer to 120°C/250°F, or in a heavy-based saucepan, to blanch the chips. Preheat the oven to 150°C/300°F/Gas Mark 2.

2 Peel the potatoes and cut into even-sized chips. Fry for about 8–10 minutes, until softened but not coloured. Remove from the oil, drain and place in a warm dish in the warm oven. Increase the temperature of the oil to 180–190°C/350–375°F.

3 Meanwhile, season the fish with salt and pepper and dust it lightly with a little flour. Make a thick batter by sieving the flour into a bowl with a little salt and whisking in most of the lager. The consistency should be very thick, like double cream.

4 Dip one fillet into the batter and allow it to be thickly coated. Carefully place the fish in the hot oil, then repeat. Cook for 8–10 minutes, depending on the thickness of the fish. Turn the fillets over halfway through the cooking time. Remove the fish from the fryer or saucepan, drain and keep warm.

5 Make sure the oil temperature is still at 180°C/350°F and return the chips to the fryer or saucepan. Cook for a further 2–3 minutes until golden brown and crispy. Drain and season with salt and pepper before serving with the battered fish and lemon wedges for squeezing over.

fisherman's pie

ingredients

SERVES 6

butter, for greasing

900 g/2 lb white fish fillets,
    such as plaice, skinned

150 ml/5 fl oz dry white wine

1 tbsp chopped fresh parsley,
    tarragon or dill

175 g/6 oz small mushrooms,
    sliced

100 g/3^{1}/$_{2}$ oz butter

175 g/6 oz cooked peeled
    prawns

40 g/1^{1}/$_{2}$ oz plain flour

125 ml/4 fl oz double cream

900 g/2 lb floury potatoes,
    such as King Edward,
    Maris Piper or Desiree,
    peeled and cut into even-
    sized chunks

salt and pepper

method

1 Preheat the oven to 180°C/350°F/Gas Mark 4. Butter a 1.7-litre/3-pint baking dish.

2 Fold the fish fillets in half and place in the dish. Season well, pour over the wine and scatter over the herbs.

3 Cover with foil and bake for 15 minutes until the fish starts to flake. Strain off the liquid and reserve for the sauce. Increase the oven temperature to 220°C/425°F/Gas Mark 7.

4 Sauté the mushrooms in a frying pan with 15 g/^{1}/$_{2}$ oz of the butter and spoon over the fish. Scatter over the prawns.

5 Heat 55 g/2 oz of the butter in a saucepan and stir in the flour. Cook for a few minutes without browning, remove from the heat, then add the reserved cooking liquid gradually, stirring well between each addition.

6 Return to the heat and gently bring to the boil, stirring constantly. Add the cream and season to taste with salt and pepper. Pour over the fish in the dish and smooth over the surface.

7 Cook the potatoes in boiling salted water for 15–20 minutes. Drain well and mash with a potato masher until smooth. Season and add the remaining butter, stirring until melted.

8 Pile the potato onto the fish and sauce and bake for 10–15 minutes until golden brown.

salmon fishcakes

ingredients

SERVES 4

700 g/1 lb 9 oz skinless
  salmon fillet,
  cut into cubes
300 ml/10 fl oz full-fat milk
1 bay leaf
100 g/3$^{1}/_{2}$ oz broccoli,
  steamed until tender
700 g/1 lb 9 oz potatoes,
  boiled and mashed
2 tbsp finely chopped fresh
  parsley
4 tbsp wholemeal plain flour
pepper
1 egg yolk
2 large eggs, beaten
150 g/5$^{1}/_{2}$ oz fresh wholemeal
  breadcrumbs
2 tbsp olive oil

method

1 Preheat the oven to 200°C/400°F/
Gas Mark 6. Put the salmon in a saucepan
with the milk and bay leaf and bring slowly
up to a simmer. Simmer for 2 minutes, then
remove the saucepan from the heat, lift out
and discard the bay leaf and leave the fish
in the milk to cool. When cooled, lift out the
fish with a slotted spoon onto kitchen paper
to drain.

2 Flake the fish into a large bowl. Put the
broccoli in a food processor and pulse until
smooth. Add to the fish with the mashed
potatoes, parsley, 1 tablespoon of the flour,
and pepper to taste. Add the egg yolk and mix
well. If the mixture is a little dry, add some
of the poaching milk; if too wet, add a little
more flour.

3 Divide the mixture into 12 portions and
shape each portion into a cake. Put the
beaten eggs, remaining flour and the
breadcrumbs on 3 separate plates. Roll
each fishcake in the flour, then in the beaten
egg, and then in the breadcrumbs to coat.

4 Heat the oil in a non-stick baking tray in
the preheated oven for 5 minutes. Add the
fishcakes and bake for 10 minutes, then
carefully turn the fishcakes over and bake for
a further 10 minutes. Serve hot.

winter vegetable cobbler

ingredients

SERVES 4

1 tbsp olive oil

1 garlic clove, crushed

8 small onions, halved

2 celery sticks, sliced

225 g/8 oz swede, chopped

2 carrots, sliced

1/2 small head of cauliflower,
    broken into florets

225 g/8 oz button
    mushrooms, sliced

400 g/14 oz canned chopped
    tomatoes

55 g/2 oz red lentils, rinsed

2 tbsp cornflour

3–4 tbsp water

300 ml/10 fl oz vegetable
    stock

2 tsp Tabasco sauce

2 tsp chopped fresh oregano

fresh oregano sprigs,
    to garnish

for the topping

225 g/8 oz self-raising flour

pinch of salt

4 tbsp butter

115 g/4 oz grated mature
    Cheddar cheese

2 tsp chopped fresh oregano

1 egg, lightly beaten

150 ml/5 fl oz milk

method

1 Preheat the oven to 180°C/350°F/Gas Mark 4. Heat the oil in a large frying pan and cook the garlic and onions over a low heat for 5 minutes. Add the celery, swede, carrots and cauliflower and cook for 2–3 minutes.

2 Add the mushrooms, tomatoes and lentils. Place the cornflour and water in a bowl and mix to make a smooth paste. Stir into the frying pan with the stock, Tabasco and oregano. Transfer to an ovenproof dish, cover and bake in the preheated oven for 20 minutes.

3 To make the topping, sift the flour and salt into a bowl. Add the butter and rub it in, then stir in most of the cheese and oregano. Beat the egg with the milk in a small bowl and add enough to the dry ingredients to make a soft dough. Knead, then roll out on a lightly floured work surface to 1 cm/1/2 inch thick. Cut into 5-cm/2-inch rounds.

4 Remove the dish from the oven and increase the temperature to 200°C/400°F/Gas Mark 6. Arrange the dough rounds around the edge of the dish, brush with the remaining egg and milk mixture and sprinkle with the reserved cheese. Cook for a further 10–12 minutes. Garnish with oregano sprigs and serve.

roasted butternut squash risotto

ingredients

SERVES 4

600 g/1 lb 5 oz butternut
  squash or pumpkin,
  peeled and cut into
  bite-sized pieces
4 tbsp olive oil
1 tsp clear honey
25 g/1 oz fresh basil, plus
  extra sprigs
  to garnish
25 g/1 oz fresh oregano
1 tbsp margarine
2 onions, finely chopped
450 g/1 lb arborio or other
  risotto rice
175 ml/6 fl oz dry white wine
1.2 litres/2 pints vegetable
  stock
salt and pepper

method

1 Preheat the oven to 200°C/400°F/
Gas Mark 6. Put the squash into a roasting
tin. Mix 1 tablespoon of the oil with the
honey and spoon over the squash. Turn
the squash to coat it in the mixture. Roast
in the preheated oven for 30–35 minutes,
or until tender.

2 Meanwhile, put the basil and oregano into
a food processor with 2 tablespoons of the
remaining oil and process until finely chopped
and blended. Set aside.

3 Heat the margarine and remaining oil
in a large, heavy-based saucepan over a
medium heat. Add the onions and fry, stirring
occasionally, for 8 minutes, or until soft and
golden. Add the rice and cook for 2 minutes,
stirring to coat the grains in the oil mixture.

4 Pour in the wine and bring to the boil.
Reduce the heat slightly and cook until the
wine is almost absorbed. Add the stock, a little
at a time, and cook over a medium-low heat,
stirring constantly, for 20 minutes.

5 Gently stir in the herb oil and squash and
cook for a further 5 minutes, or until the rice is
cooked but retaining a little bite in the centre
of the grain. Season well before serving,
garnished with basil.

macaroni cheese

ingredients

SERVES 4

600 ml/1 pint milk

1 onion, peeled

8 peppercorns

1 bay leaf

55 g/2 oz butter

40 g/1$\frac{1}{2}$ oz plain flour

$\frac{1}{2}$ tsp ground nutmeg

5 tbsp double cream

pepper

100 g/3$\frac{1}{2}$ oz mature Cheddar
   cheese, grated

100 g/3$\frac{1}{2}$ oz Roquefort
   cheese, crumbled

350 g/12 oz dried macaroni

100 g/3$\frac{1}{2}$ oz Gruyère or
   Emmental cheese, grated

method

1 Put the milk, onion, peppercorns and bay leaf in a pan and bring to the boil. Remove from the heat and let stand for 15 minutes.

2 Melt the butter in a pan and stir in the flour until well combined and smooth. Cook over a medium heat, stirring constantly, for 1 minute. Remove from the heat. Strain the milk to remove the solids and stir a little into the butter and flour mixture until well incorporated. Return to the heat and gradually add the remaining milk, stirring constantly, until it has all been incorporated. Cook for a further 3 minutes, or until the sauce is smooth and thickened, then add the nutmeg, cream and pepper to taste. Add the Cheddar and Roquefort cheeses and stir until melted.

3 Meanwhile, bring a large pan of water to the boil. Add the macaroni, then return to the boil and cook for 8–10 minutes, or until just tender. Drain well and add to the cheese sauce. Stir well together.

4 Preheat the grill to high. Spoon the mixture into an ovenproof serving dish, then scatter over the Gruyère cheese and cook under the grill until bubbling and brown.

souffléd baked potatoes

ingredients

SERVES 4

2 baking potatoes, scrubbed

1 tbsp olive oil

2 tbsp full-fat milk

25 g/1 oz butter

25 g/1 oz Cheddar or Gruyère
   cheese, grated

1 large egg, separated

2 slices ham, cooked turkey
   or unsmoked bacon,
   chopped

2 tbsp finely grated Parmesan
   cheese

salt and pepper

salad, to serve

method

1 Preheat the oven to 200°C/400°F/ Gas Mark 6. Prick the potatoes with a fork. Rub the oil all over the potatoes, place on a baking sheet and bake in the preheated oven for 1 hour, or until the flesh is soft.

2 Remove the potatoes from the oven, cut in half lengthways and carefully scoop out the flesh into a bowl, keeping the skins intact. Set the skins aside.

3 Add the milk, butter, Cheddar cheese and egg yolk to the potato and mash well. Season to taste with salt and pepper. Mix in the ham.

4 In a separate, grease-free bowl, whisk the egg white until stiff, then fold into the potato mixture.

5 Pile the potato mixture back into the skins and sprinkle over the Parmesan cheese. Return to the oven and bake for 20 minutes. Serve with salad.

perfect mash

ingredients

SERVES 4

900 g/2 lb floury potatoes,
  such as King Edward,
  Maris Piper or Desiree
4 tbsp butter
3 tbsp hot milk
salt and pepper

method

1 Peel the potatoes, placing them in cold water as you prepare the others to prevent them from going brown.

2 Cut the potatoes into even-sized chunks and cook in a large saucepan of boiling salted water over a medium heat, covered, for 20–25 minutes until they are tender. Test with the point of a knife, but make sure you test right in the middle to avoid lumps.

3 Remove the pan from the heat and drain the potatoes. Return the potatoes to the hot pan and mash with a potato masher until smooth.

4 Add the butter and continue to mash until it is all mixed in, then add the milk (it is better hot because the potatoes absorb it more quickly to produce a creamier mash).

5 Taste the mashed potatoes and season with salt and pepper as necessary. Serve at once.

cauliflower cheese

ingredients

SERVES 4

1 cauliflower, trimmed and
   cut into florets (675 g/
    1 lb 8 oz prepared weight)
40 g/1^1/$_2$ oz butter
40 g/1^1/$_2$ oz plain flour
450 ml/16 fl oz milk
115 g/4 oz Cheddar cheese,
   finely grated
whole nutmeg, for grating
1 tbsp grated Parmesan
   cheese
salt and pepper

method

1 Cook the cauliflower in a saucepan of boiling salted water for 4–5 minutes. It should still be firm. Drain, place in a hot 1.4-litre/2^1/$_2$-pint gratin dish and keep warm.

2 Melt the butter in the rinsed-out saucepan over a medium heat and stir in the flour. Cook for 1 minute, stirring constantly.

3 Remove from the heat and stir in the milk gradually until you have a smooth consistency.

4 Return to a low heat and continue to stir while the sauce comes to the boil and thickens. Reduce the heat and simmer gently, stirring constantly, for about 3 minutes until the sauce is creamy and smooth.

5 Remove from the heat and stir in the Cheddar cheese and a good grating of the nutmeg. Taste and season well with salt and pepper.

6 Pour the hot sauce over the cauliflower, top with the Parmesan and place under a hot grill to brown. Serve immediately.

Granny's
travels

Grannys in this day and age are jetting off or cruising all over the world. Travel is cheaper and easier than in the past, making it possible to visit far-off destinations with diverse cultures and foods. Countries like China, Mexico and the newly accessible Eastern European nations have all contributed to our varied cuisine.

We have taken recipes from many different cultures and adapted them to our own way of eating. As our society becomes increasingly multicultural, ingredients for these types of recipes are becoming more readily available, not just from specialist shops but increasingly from main-stream supermarkets. Pasta has long been a favourite and spaghetti Bolognese is popular with adults and children alike. Pizza is an ideal finger food that can be made from scratch or using prepared pizza bases and topped with different ingredients so that everyone can choose their own. From further afield come chicken Kiev and beef goulash, together with chicken fajitas and chilli con carne, introducing newer flavours and spices into our diets. Chow mein and Chinese spare ribs, with their use of eastern flavours and foodstuffs, are also included in this chapter.

spaghetti bolognese

ingredients

SERVES 4

1 tbsp olive oil

1 onion, finely chopped

2 garlic cloves, chopped

1 carrot, chopped

1 celery stick, chopped

50 g/1¾ oz pancetta or
   streaky bacon, diced

350 g/12 oz lean fresh beef
   mince

400 g/14 oz canned chopped
   tomatoes

2 tsp dried oregano

125 ml/4 fl oz red wine

2 tbsp tomato purée

350 g/12 oz dried spaghetti

salt and pepper

freshly grated Parmesan
   cheese, to serve (optional)

method

1 Heat the oil in a large frying pan over a low heat. Add the onion and cook for 3 minutes.

2 Add the garlic, carrot, celery and pancetta to the pan and sauté for 3–4 minutes, or until just starting to brown.

3 Add the beef and cook over a high heat for another 3 minutes, or until the meat has browned.

4 Stir in the tomatoes, oregano and red wine and bring to the boil. Reduce the heat and simmer for about 45 minutes.

5 Stir in the tomato purée and season with salt and pepper.

6 Bring a large pan of lightly salted water to the boil over a medium heat. Add the pasta and cook for about 8–10 minutes, or until tender, but still firm to the bite. Drain thoroughly.

7 Transfer the pasta to 4 serving plates and pour over the sauce. Toss to mix well and serve with Parmesan cheese, if you wish.

spaghetti with meatballs

ingredients

SERVES 6

1 potato, diced

400 g/14 oz fresh beef mince

1 onion, finely chopped

1 egg

4 tbsp chopped fresh flat-leaf
    parsley

plain flour, for dusting

5 tbsp olive oil

400 ml/14 fl oz passata

2 tbsp tomato purée

450 g/1 lb dried spaghetti

salt and pepper

6 fresh basil leaves, shredded,
    plus Parmesan cheese
    shavings, to garnish

method

1 Place the potato in a small pan, add cold water to cover and a pinch of salt and bring to the boil. Cook for 10–15 minutes, until tender, then drain. Either mash thoroughly with a potato masher or fork or pass through a potato ricer.

2 Combine the potato, beef, onion, egg and parsley in a bowl and season to taste with salt and pepper. Spread out the flour on a plate. With dampened hands, shape the meat mixture into walnut-size balls and roll in the flour. Shake off any excess.

3 Heat the oil in a heavy-based frying pan, add the meatballs and cook over a medium heat, stirring and turning frequently, for 8–10 minutes, until golden all over.

4 Add the passata and tomato purée and cook for a further 10 minutes, until the sauce is reduced and thickened.

5 Meanwhile, bring a large saucepan of lightly salted water to the boil. Add the pasta, bring back to the boil and cook for 8–10 minutes, until tender, but still firm to the bite.

6 Drain well and add to the meatball sauce, tossing well to coat. Transfer to a warm serving dish, garnish with the basil leaves and Parmesan and serve immediately.

fettuccine alfredo

ingredients

SERVES 4

2 tbsp butter

200 ml/7 fl oz double cream

450 g/1 lb fresh fettuccine

85 g/3 oz freshly grated
   Parmesan cheese, plus
   extra to serve

pinch of freshly grated
   nutmeg

salt and pepper

fresh flat-leaf parsley sprigs,
   to garnish

method

1 Put the butter and 150 ml/5 fl oz of the cream into a large pan and bring the mixture to the boil over a medium heat. Reduce the heat, then simmer gently for $1^{1}/2$ minutes, or until the cream has thickened slightly.

2 Meanwhile, bring a large pan of lightly salted water to the boil over medium heat. Add the pasta and cook for 2–3 minutes, or until tender, but still firm to the bite. Drain thoroughly and return to the pan, then pour over the cream sauce.

3 Toss the pasta in the sauce over a low heat, stirring with a wooden spoon, until coated thoroughly.

4 Add the remaining cream, Parmesan cheese and nutmeg to the pasta mixture and season to taste with salt and pepper. Toss the pasta in the mixture while heating through.

5 Transfer the pasta mixture to warmed serving bowls and garnish with fresh parsley sprigs. Serve immediately with extra grated Parmesan cheese.

lasagne al forno

ingredients

SERVES 4

2 tbsp olive oil

55 g/2 oz pancetta or rindless
    streaky bacon, chopped

1 onion, chopped

1 garlic clove, finely chopped

225 g/8 oz fresh beef mince

2 celery sticks, chopped

2 carrots, chopped

pinch of sugar

$1/2$ tsp dried oregano

400 g/14 oz canned chopped
    tomatoes

350 ml/12 fl oz shop-bought
    cheese sauce

225 g/8 oz dried no-precook
    lasagne sheets

115 g/4 oz freshly grated
    Parmesan cheese, plus
    extra for sprinkling

salt and pepper

method

1 Preheat the oven to 190°C/375°F/Gas
Mark 5. Heat the olive oil in a large, heavy-
based saucepan. Add the pancetta and cook
over a medium heat, stirring occasionally,
for 3 minutes, or until the fat begins to run.
Add the onion and garlic and cook, stirring
occasionally, for 5 minutes, or until softened.

2 Add the beef and cook, breaking it up with
a wooden spoon, until browned all over. Stir in
the celery and carrots and cook for 5 minutes.
Season to taste with salt and pepper. Add
the sugar, oregano and tomatoes. Bring to
the boil, reduce the heat and simmer for
30 minutes. Gently heat the cheese sauce.
Keep warm.

3 In a large, rectangular ovenproof dish, make
alternate layers of meat sauce, lasagne and
Parmesan cheese. Pour the cheese sauce
over the layers, covering them completely, and
sprinkle with Parmesan cheese. Bake in the
preheated oven for 30 minutes, or until golden
brown and bubbling. Serve immediately.

pizza margherita

ingredients

SERVES 4

for the pizza dough

15 g/^{1}/$_2$ oz easy-blend dried
    yeast
1 tsp sugar
250 ml/9 fl oz warm water
350 g/12 oz strong white
    flour, plus extra for dusting
1 tsp salt
1 tbsp olive oil, plus extra
    for oiling

for the topping

400 g/14 oz canned chopped
    tomatoes
2 garlic cloves, crushed
2 tsp dried basil
1 tbsp olive oil
2 tbsp tomato purée
100 g/3^1/$_2$ oz mozzarella
    cheese, chopped
2 tbsp freshly grated
    Parmesan cheese
salt and pepper

method

1 Place the yeast and sugar in a measuring jug and mix with 50 ml/2 fl oz of the water. Leave the yeast mixture in a warm place for 15 minutes or until frothy.

2 Mix the flour with the salt and make a well in the centre. Add the oil, the yeast mixture and the remaining water. Using a wooden spoon, mix to form a smooth dough.

3 Turn the dough out onto a floured surface and knead for 4–5 minutes or until smooth. Return the dough to the bowl, cover with an oiled sheet of clingfilm and leave to rise for 30 minutes or until doubled in size.

4 Knead the dough for 2 minutes. Stretch the dough with your hands, then place it on an oiled baking tray, pushing out the edges until even. The dough should be no more than 6 mm/^{1}/$_4$ inch thick.

5 Preheat the oven to 200°C/400°F/Gas Mark 6. To make the topping, place the tomatoes, garlic, dried basil, olive oil and salt and pepper to taste in a large frying pan and leave to simmer for 20 minutes or until the sauce has thickened. Stir in the tomato purée and leave to cool slightly.

6 Spread the topping evenly over the pizza base. Top with the cheeses and bake in the preheated oven for 20–25 minutes. Serve hot.

ratatouille

ingredients

SERVES 4

2 aubergines

4 courgettes

2 yellow peppers

2 red peppers

2 onions

2 garlic cloves

150 ml/5 fl oz olive oil

1 bouquet garni

3 large tomatoes, peeled,
    deseeded and roughly
    chopped

salt and pepper

method

1 Roughly chop the aubergines and courgettes, and deseed and chop the peppers. Slice the onions and finely chop the garlic. Heat the oil in a large saucepan. Add the onions and cook over a low heat, stirring occasionally, for 5 minutes, or until softened. Add the garlic and cook, stirring frequently for a further 2 minutes.

2 Add the aubergines, courgettes and peppers. Increase the heat to medium and cook, stirring occasionally, until the peppers begin to colour. Add the bouquet garni, reduce the heat, cover and simmer gently for 40 minutes.

3 Stir in the chopped tomatoes and season to taste with salt and pepper. Re-cover the saucepan and simmer gently for a further 10 minutes. Remove and discard the bouquet garni. Serve warm or cold.

paella

ingredients

SERVES 4

3 tbsp olive oil

2 tbsp butter

2 garlic cloves, chopped

1 onion, chopped

2 large tomatoes, deseeded
   and diced

85 g/3 oz frozen peas

1 red pepper, deseeded and
   chopped

150 g/5$^1/_2$ oz arborio rice

2 tsp dried mixed herbs

1 tsp saffron powder

425 ml/15 fl oz chicken stock

4 skinless, boneless chicken
   breasts

150 g/5$^1/_2$ oz lean chorizo,
   skinned

200 g/7 oz cooked lobster
   meat

200 g/7 oz prawns, peeled
   and deveined

1 tbsp chopped fresh flat-leaf
   parsley

salt and pepper

to garnish

pinch of cayenne pepper

red pepper strips

method

1 Heat the oil and butter in a large frying pan over a medium heat. Add the garlic and onion and cook, stirring, for 3 minutes, or until slightly softened.

2 Add the tomatoes, peas, red pepper, rice, mixed herbs and saffron and cook, stirring, for 2 minutes. Pour in the stock and bring to the boil. Reduce the heat to low and cook, stirring, for 10 minutes.

3 Chop the chicken into bite-sized pieces and add to the frying pan. Cook, stirring occasionally, for 5 minutes. Chop up the chorizo, add to the frying pan and cook for 3 minutes. Chop up the lobster meat and add to the pan with the prawns and parsley. Season with salt and pepper and cook, stirring, for a further 2 minutes.

4 Remove the frying pan from the heat, transfer the paella to a large serving platter or individual plates, garnish with cayenne and red pepper strips and serve.

coq au vin

ingredients

SERVES 4

4 tbsp butter

2 tbsp olive oil

1.8 kg/4 lb chicken pieces

115 g/4 oz rindless smoked
     bacon, cut into strips

115 g/4 oz baby onions

115 g/4 oz chestnut
     mushrooms, halved

2 garlic cloves, finely chopped

2 tbsp brandy

225 ml/8 fl oz red wine

300 ml/10 fl oz chicken stock

1 bouquet garni

2 tbsp plain flour

salt and pepper

bay leaves, to garnish

method

1 Melt half the butter with the olive oil in a large, flameproof casserole. Add the chicken and cook over a medium heat, stirring, for 8–10 minutes, or until golden brown all over. Add the bacon, onions, mushrooms and garlic.

2 Pour in the brandy and set it alight with a match or taper. When the flames have died down, add the wine, stock and bouquet garni and season to taste with salt and pepper. Bring to the boil, reduce the heat and simmer gently for 1 hour, or until the chicken pieces are cooked through and tender. Meanwhile, make a beurre manié by mashing the remaining butter with the flour in a small bowl.

3 Remove and discard the bouquet garni. Transfer the chicken to a large plate and keep warm. Stir the beurre manié into the casserole, a little at a time. Bring to the boil, return the chicken to the casserole and serve immediately, garnished with bay leaves.

rich beef stew

ingredients

SERVES 4

1 tbsp oil

1 tbsp butter

225 g/8 oz baby onions,
   peeled and halved

600 g/1 lb 5 oz stewing steak,
   diced into 4-cm/1^1/$_2$-inch
   chunks

300 ml/10 fl oz beef stock

150 ml/5 fl oz red wine

4 tbsp chopped fresh oregano

1 tbsp sugar

1 orange

25 g/1 oz dried porcini or
   other dried mushrooms

4 tbsp warm water

225 g/8 oz fresh plum
   tomatoes

cooked rice or potatoes,
   to serve

method

1 Preheat the oven to 180°C/350°F/Gas Mark 4. Heat the oil and butter in a large frying pan. Add the onions and cook for 5 minutes, or until golden. Remove with a slotted spoon, set aside and keep warm.

2 Add the beef to the frying pan and cook, stirring, for 5 minutes, or until browned all over.

3 Return the onions to the frying pan and add the stock, wine, oregano and sugar, stirring to mix well. Transfer the mixture to an ovenproof casserole.

4 Pare the rind from the orange and cut it into strips. Slice the orange flesh into rings. Add the orange rings and the rind to the casserole. Cook in the oven for 1^1/4 hours.

5 Soak the mushrooms for 30 minutes in a small bowl containing the warm water.

6 Peel and halve the tomatoes. Add the tomatoes, mushrooms and their soaking liquid to the casserole. Cook for a further 20 minutes, or until the beef is tender and the juices have thickened. Serve with rice or potatoes.

chilli con carne

ingredients

SERVES 4

1 tbsp sunflower or corn oil

1 small onion, roughly
  chopped

1 or 2 garlic cloves, roughly
  chopped

1 green pepper, deseeded
  and diced

225 g/8 oz fresh beef mince

1 tsp chilli powder

400 g/14 oz canned chopped
  tomatoes

$1/2$ tsp salt (optional)

400 g/14 oz canned kidney
  beans, drained and rinsed

to serve

grated cheese

freshly cooked rice

tortilla chips

method

1 Heat the oil in a shallow frying pan over a low heat. Stir in the onion, garlic and green pepper and cook gently for 5 minutes.

2 Add the beef mince and stir well. Increase the heat to high and cook for 5 minutes, stirring occasionally. Spoon off any excess fat. Sprinkle over the chilli powder and mix well. Continue cooking for 2–3 minutes. Stir in the tomatoes, reduce the heat, cover and cook gently for at least 30 minutes. You may need to add a little water or beef stock if it starts to dry out.

3 Halfway through the cooking time, check the seasoning and stir in the salt if needed. Add more chilli powder to taste, but be careful not to use too much.

4 Add the drained kidney beans to the chilli mixture 5–10 minutes before the end of the cooking time so that they heat through with the meat and spices.

5 Serve immediately topped with a little grated cheese and accompanied by freshly cooked rice and tortilla chips.

chicken fajitas

ingredients

SERVES 4

3 tbsp olive oil, plus extra for drizzling

3 tbsp maple syrup or clear honey

1 tbsp red wine vinegar

2 garlic cloves, crushed

2 tsp dried oregano

1–2 tsp dried red chilli flakes

4 chicken breasts, skinless, boneless

2 red peppers, deseeded and cut into 2.5-cm/1-inch strips

8 flour tortillas, warmed

salt and pepper

method

1 Place the oil, maple syrup, vinegar, garlic, oregano, chilli flakes and salt and pepper to taste in a large, shallow dish or bowl and mix together.

2 Slice the chicken across the grain into slices 2.5 cm/1 inch thick. Toss in the marinade until well coated. Cover and leave to chill in the refrigerator for 2–3 hours, turning occasionally.

3 Heat a griddle pan until hot. Lift the chicken slices from the marinade with a slotted spoon, lay on the griddle pan and cook over a medium-high heat for 3–4 minutes on each side, or until cooked through. Remove the chicken to a warmed serving plate and keep warm.

4 Add the peppers, skin side down, to the griddle pan and cook for 2 minutes on each side. Transfer to the serving plate.

5 Serve immediately with the warmed tortillas to be used as wraps.

chicken tikka masala

ingredients

SERVES 6

$1/2$ onion, roughly chopped

55 g/2 oz tomato purée

1 tsp cumin seeds

2.5-cm/1-inch piece fresh
 root ginger, chopped

3 tbsp lemon juice

2 garlic cloves, crushed

2 tsp chilli powder

750 g/1 lb 10 oz boneless
 chicken

salt and pepper

fresh mint sprigs, to garnish

for the masala sauce

2 tbsp ghee

1 onion, sliced

1 tbsp black onion seeds

3 garlic cloves, crushed

2 fresh green chillies,
 chopped

200 g/7 oz canned chopped
 tomatoes

125 ml/4 fl oz low-fat natural
 yogurt

125 ml/4 fl oz coconut milk

1 tbsp chopped fresh
 coriander

1 tbsp chopped fresh mint

2 tbsp lemon or lime juice

$1/2$ tsp garam masala

method

1 Combine the onion, tomato purée, cumin seeds, ginger, lemon juice, garlic and chilli powder in a food processor or blender and transfer to a bowl. Season to taste with salt and pepper. Cut the chicken into 4-cm/ $11/2$-inch cubes. Stir into the bowl and leave for 2 hours.

2 Make the masala sauce. Heat the ghee in a saucepan, add the onion and stir over a medium heat for 5 minutes. Add the black onion seeds, garlic and chillies. Add the tomatoes, yogurt and coconut milk, bring to the boil, then simmer for 20 minutes.

3 Divide the chicken evenly between 8 oiled skewers and cook under a very hot preheated grill for 15 minutes, turning frequently. Remove the chicken and add to the sauce. Stir in the herbs, lemon juice and garam masala. Serve garnished with mint sprigs.

vegetable korma

ingredients

SERVES 4

4 tbsp ghee or vegetable oil

2 onions, chopped

2 garlic cloves, chopped

1 fresh red chilli, chopped

1 tbsp grated fresh root ginger

2 tomatoes, peeled and
    chopped

1 orange pepper, deseeded
    and cut into small pieces

1 large potato, cut into
    chunks

200 g/7 oz cauliflower florets

$^{1}/_{2}$ tsp salt

1 tsp ground turmeric

1 tsp ground cumin

1 tsp ground coriander

1 tsp garam masala

200 ml/7 fl oz vegetable stock
    or water

150 ml/5 fl oz natural yogurt

150 ml/5 fl oz single cream

25 g/1 oz fresh coriander,
    chopped

freshly cooked rice, to serve

method

1 Heat the ghee in a large saucepan over a medium heat, add the onions and garlic and cook, stirring, for 3 minutes. Add the chilli and ginger and cook for a further 4 minutes. Add the tomatoes, pepper, potato, cauliflower, salt and spices and cook, stirring, for a further 3 minutes. Stir in the stock and bring to the boil. Reduce the heat and simmer for 25 minutes.

2 Stir in the yogurt and cream and cook, stirring, for a further 5 minutes. Add the fresh coriander and heat through.

3 Serve the curry with freshly cooked rice.

chicken kiev

ingredients

SERVES 4

4 tbsp butter, softened

1 garlic clove, finely chopped

1 tbsp finely chopped fresh
    parsley, plus extra sprigs
    to garnish

1 tbsp finely chopped fresh
    oregano

4 skinless, boneless chicken
    breasts

85 g/3 oz fresh white or
    wholemeal breadcrumbs

3 tbsp freshly grated
    Parmesan cheese

1 egg, beaten

250 ml/9 fl oz vegetable oil,
    for deep-frying

salt and pepper

freshly cooked new potatoes
    and a selection of cooked
    vegetables, to serve

method

1 Place the butter and garlic in a bowl and mix together well. Stir in the chopped herbs and season well with salt and pepper. Pound the chicken breasts to flatten them to an even thickness, then place a tablespoon of herb butter in the centre of each one. Fold in the sides to enclose the butter, then secure with cocktail sticks.

2 Combine the breadcrumbs and grated Parmesan on a plate. Dip the chicken parcels into the beaten egg, then coat in the breadcrumb mixture. Transfer to a plate, cover and chill for 30 minutes. Remove from the refrigerator and coat in the egg and then the breadcrumb mixture for a second time.

3 Pour the oil into a deep-fat fryer to a depth that will cover the chicken parcels. Heat until it reaches 180–190°C/350–375°F, or until a cube of bread browns in 30 seconds. Transfer the chicken to the hot oil and deep-fry for 5 minutes, or until cooked through. Lift out the chicken and drain on kitchen paper.

4 Divide the chicken among 4 serving plates, garnish with parsley sprigs and serve with new potatoes and a selection of vegetables.

beef goulash

ingredients

SERVES 4

2 tbsp vegetable oil

1 large onion, chopped

1 garlic clove, crushed

750 g/1 lb 10 oz lean braising
beef

2 tbsp paprika

400 g/14 oz canned chopped
tomatoes

2 tbsp tomato purée

1 large red pepper, deseeded
and chopped

175 g/6 oz button
mushrooms, sliced

600 ml/1 pint beef stock

1 tbsp cornflour

1 tbsp water

salt and pepper

chopped fresh parsley,
to garnish

freshly cooked long-grain and
wild rice, to serve

method

1 Heat the vegetable oil in a large, heavy-based frying pan. Add the onion and garlic and cook over a low heat for 3–4 minutes.

2 Using a sharp knife, cut the beef into chunks, add to the frying pan and cook over a high heat for 3 minutes, or until browned. Add the paprika and stir well, then add the tomatoes, tomato purée, red pepper and mushrooms. Cook for a further 2 minutes, stirring frequently. Pour in the stock. Bring to the boil, reduce the heat, cover and simmer for 1¹/₂–2 hours, or until the meat is tender.

3 Blend the cornflour and water together in a small bowl, then add to the frying pan, stirring, until thickened and smooth. Cook for 1 minute. Season to taste with salt and pepper.

4 Transfer the beef goulash to a warmed serving dish, garnish with chopped fresh parsley and serve with a mix of long-grain and wild rice.

mushroom stroganoff

ingredients

SERVES 4

550 g/1 lb 4 oz mixed fresh
    mushrooms, such as
    chanterelles, chestnut,
    ceps and oyster
1 red onion, diced
2 garlic cloves, crushed
425 ml/15 fl oz vegetable
    stock
1 tbsp tomato purée
2 tbsp lemon juice
15 g/$^1/_2$ oz cornflour
2 tbsp cold water
115 g/4 oz low-fat natural
    yogurt
2 tbsp chopped fresh parsley,
    plus extra to garnish
pepper
freshly cooked brown or white
    rice, to serve

method

1 Put the mushrooms, onion, garlic, stock, tomato purée and lemon juice into a saucepan and bring to the boil. Reduce the heat, cover and simmer for 15 minutes, or until the onion is tender.

2 Blend the cornflour with the water in a small bowl and stir into the mushroom mixture. Return to the boil, stirring constantly, and cook until the sauce thickens. Reduce the heat and simmer for a further 2–3 minutes, stirring occasionally.

3 Just before serving, remove the saucepan from the heat and stir in the yogurt, making sure that the stroganoff is not boiling or it may separate and curdle. Stir in 2 tablespoons of the parsley and season to taste with pepper. Transfer the stroganoff to a warmed serving dish, sprinkle over the remaining parsley and serve immediately with freshly cooked brown or white rice.

sweet & sour prawns

ingredients

SERVES 4

450 g/1 lb cooked tiger
    prawns
1 tbsp groundnut or
    sunflower oil
4 spring onions, finely
    chopped
2 tsp finely chopped fresh
    root ginger
2 tbsp dark soy sauce
2 tbsp muscovado sugar
3 tbsp rice vinegar
1 tbsp Chinese rice wine
125 ml/4 fl oz fish or chicken
    stock
1 tsp cornflour
1–2 tbsp water
dash of sesame oil
shredded spring onion,
    to garnish
shredded Chinese leaves,
    to serve

method

1 Peel and devein the prawns, pat dry with kitchen paper and reserve.

2 Heat the oil in a preheated wok or large frying pan. Add the spring onions and ginger and stir-fry over a high heat for 1 minute. Add the soy sauce, sugar, vinegar, rice wine and stock and bring to the boil.

3 Place the cornflour and water in a small bowl and mix to make a paste. Stir 1 tablespoon of the paste into the sauce and add the prawns. Cook, stirring, until slightly thickened and smooth. Sprinkle with sesame oil.

4 Make a bed of Chinese leaves in 4 serving bowls and top with the prawns and sauce. Garnish with the shredded spring onion and serve immediately.

pork chow mein

ingredients

SERVES 4

250 g/9 oz egg noodles

4–5 tbsp vegetable oil

250 g/9 oz pork fillet, cooked

125 g/4^{1}/$_{2}$ oz French beans

2 tbsp light soy sauce

1 tsp salt

^{1}/$_{2}$ tsp sugar

1 tbsp Chinese rice wine or
   dry sherry

2 spring onions, finely
   shredded

a few drops sesame oil

chilli sauce, to serve
   (optional)

method

1 Cook the noodles in boiling water according to the instructions on the packet, then drain and rinse under cold water. Drain again then toss with 1 tablespoon of the oil.

2 Slice the pork into thin shreds and trim the beans.

3 Heat 3 tablespoons of the oil in a preheated wok until hot. Add the noodles and stir-fry for 2–3 minutes with 1 tablespoon of the soy sauce, then remove to a serving dish. Keep warm.

4 Heat the remaining oil and stir-fry the beans and meat for 2 minutes. Add the salt, sugar, rice wine, the remaining soy sauce and about half of the spring onions to the wok.

5 Stir the mixture in the wok, adding a little stock if necessary, then pour on top of the noodles, and sprinkle with sesame oil and the remaining spring onions.

6 Serve the chow mein hot or cold with chilli sauce, if using.

chinese spare ribs

ingredients

SERVES 4

1 kg/2 lb 4 oz pork spare ribs, separated

4 tbsp dark soy sauce

3 tbsp muscovado sugar

1 tbsp groundnut or sunflower oil

2 garlic cloves, finely chopped

2 tsp Chinese five-spice powder

1-cm/^{1}/$_2$-inch piece fresh root ginger, grated

shredded spring onions, to garnish

method

1 Place the spare ribs in a large, shallow, non-metallic dish. Mix the soy sauce, sugar, oil, garlic, Chinese five-spice powder and ginger together in a bowl. Pour the mixture over the ribs and turn until the ribs are thoroughly coated in the marinade.

2 Cover the dish with clingfilm and leave to marinate in the refrigerator for at least 6 hours.

3 Preheat the barbecue. Drain the ribs, reserving the marinade. Cook over medium-hot coals, turning and brushing frequently with the reserved marinade, for 30–40 minutes. Transfer to a large serving dish, garnish with the shredded spring onions and serve immediately.

Granny's
festive fare

Christmas and other holidays were always when Granny came into her own. She would love having her family around her and always pulled out all the stops to give them the best of everything. Starters of special soups and pâté are included in this chapter and there are, of course, recipes for roast turkey and the all-important stuffing.

Gammon, goose and beef wellington recipes are also provided as alternatives to the turkey but they are just as good for winter dinners – and the salmon dish is ideal for a summer's day too. Vegetarians are not forgotten as there is a mixed nut roast to be served with a cranberry and red wine sauce, and some delicious individual vegetable dishes too. Those with a sweet tooth will not be disappointed either, as there are two very special desserts to choose from – either the customary Christmas pudding or a festive sherry trifle. These recipes can be used at other times of the year to celebrate any festival in the calendar or special family event, like a birth, christening or birthday.

wild mushroom & sherry soup

ingredients

SERVES 4

2 tbsp olive oil

1 onion, chopped

1 garlic clove, chopped

125 g/4^1/$_2$ oz sweet potato,
    peeled and chopped

1 leek, trimmed and sliced

200 g/7 oz chestnut
    mushrooms

150 g/5^1/$_2$ oz mixed wild
    mushrooms

600 ml/1 pint vegetable stock

350 ml/12 fl oz single cream

4 tbsp sherry

salt and pepper

to garnish/serve

Parmesan cheese shavings

sautéed sliced wild
    mushrooms

fresh crusty bread

method

1 Heat the oil in a saucepan over a medium heat. Add the onion and garlic and cook, stirring, for 3 minutes until softened slightly. Add the sweet potato and cook for another 3 minutes. Stir in the leek and cook for another 2 minutes.

2 Stir in the mushrooms, stock and cream. Bring to the boil, then reduce the heat and simmer gently, stirring occasionally, for about 25 minutes. Remove from the heat, stir in the sherry, and leave to cool a little.

3 Transfer half of the soup into a food processor and blend until smooth. Return the mixture to the pan with the rest of the soup, season with salt and pepper and reheat gently, stirring. Pour into 4 warmed soup bowls, garnish with Parmesan shavings and sautéed wild mushrooms, and serve with fresh crusty bread.

spiced pumpkin soup

ingredients

SERVES 4

2 tbsp olive oil

1 onion, chopped

1 garlic clove, chopped

1 tbsp chopped fresh root
   ginger

1 small red chilli, deseeded
   and finely chopped

2 tbsp chopped fresh
   coriander

1 bay leaf

1 kg/2 lb 4 oz pumpkin,
   peeled, deseeded and
   diced

600 ml/1 pint vegetable stock

salt and pepper

single cream, to garnish

method

1 Heat the oil in a saucepan over a medium heat. Add the onion and garlic and cook, stirring, for about 4 minutes, until slightly softened. Add the ginger, chilli, coriander, bay leaf and pumpkin and cook for another 3 minutes.

2 Pour in the stock and bring to the boil. Using a slotted spoon, skim any scum from the surface. Reduce the heat and simmer gently, stirring occasionally, for about 25 minutes, or until the pumpkin is tender. Remove from the heat, take out the bay leaf and leave to cool a little.

3 Transfer the soup into a food processor and blend until smooth (you may have to do this in batches). Return the mixture to the pan and season with salt and pepper. Reheat gently, stirring. Remove from the heat, pour into 4 warmed soup bowls, garnish each one with a swirl of cream and serve.

chicken liver pâté

ingredients

SERVES 4–6

200 g/7 oz butter

225 g/8 oz trimmed chicken
    livers, thawed if frozen

2 tbsp Marsala or brandy

$1^1/2$ tsp chopped fresh sage

1 garlic clove, coarsely
    chopped

150 ml/5 fl oz double cream

salt and pepper

fresh bay leaves or sage
    leaves, to garnish

crackers, to serve

method

1 Melt 40 g/1$^1/2$ oz of the butter in a large,
heavy-based frying pan. Add the chicken
livers and cook over a medium heat for about
4 minutes on each side. They should be
browned on the outside but still pink in the
middle. Transfer to a food processor and
process until finely chopped.

2 Stir the Marsala or brandy into the pan,
scraping up any sediment with a wooden
spoon, then add to the food processor with
the chopped sage, garlic and 100 g/3$^1/2$ oz of
the remaining butter. Process until smooth.
Add the cream, season with salt and pepper
and process until thoroughly combined
and smooth. Spoon the pâté into a dish or
individual ramekins, smooth the surface and
leave to cool completely.

3 Melt the remaining butter, then spoon it
over the surface of the pâté. Decorate with
herb leaves, cool, then chill in the refrigerator.
Serve with crackers.

stilton & walnut tartlets

ingredients

MAKES 12

butter, for greasing

225 g/8 oz plain flour, plus
   extra for dusting

pinch of celery salt

100 g/3^1/$_2$ oz cold butter,
   cut into pieces, plus extra
   for greasing

25 g/1 oz walnut halves,
   chopped in a food
   processor

cold water

for the filling

25 g/1 oz butter

2 celery sticks, trimmed and
   finely chopped

1 small leek, trimmed and
   finely chopped

200 ml/7 fl oz double cream,
   plus 2 tbsp extra

200 g/7 oz Stilton

3 egg yolks

salt and pepper

method

1 Lightly butter a 7.5-cm/3-inch, 12-hole muffin tray. Sift the flour and celery salt into a food processor, add the butter and process until the mixture resembles fine breadcrumbs. Tip the mixture into a large bowl and add the walnuts and a little cold water. Turn out onto a floured surface and cut the dough in half. Roll out the first piece and cut out six 9-cm/3^1/$_2$-inch circles. Take each circle and roll out to 12 cm/4^1/$_2$ inches diameter and fit into the muffin holes. Do the same with the remaining dough. Put a piece of baking paper in each hole, fill with baking beans then put the tray in the refrigerator for 30 minutes. Meanwhile, preheat the oven to 200°C/400°F/Gas Mark 6.

2 Remove the muffin tray from the refrigerator and bake the tartlets blind for 10 minutes in the preheated oven then carefully remove the paper and beans.

3 For the filling, melt the butter in a frying pan and add the celery and leek. Cook for 15 minutes, until soft. Add 2 tablespoons of the double cream and crumble in the Stilton. Mix well and season. Bring the remaining cream to a simmer in another pan, then pour on to the egg yolks, stirring constantly. Mix in the Stilton mixture and spoon into the pastry cases. Bake for 10 minutes then turn the tray around in the oven and bake for a further 5 minutes. Cool for 5 minutes before serving.

roast turkey with stuffing

ingredients

SERVES 8

1 x 5-kg/11-lb turkey

55 g/2 oz butter

5 tbsp red wine

400 ml/14 fl oz chicken stock

1 tbsp cornflour

1 tsp French mustard

1 tsp sherry vinegar

for the stuffing

225 g/8 oz pork sausagemeat

225 g/8 oz unsweetened
   chestnut purée

85 g/3 oz walnuts

115 g/4 oz dried apricots,
   chopped

2 tbsp chopped fresh parsley

2 tbsp chopped fresh chives

2 tsp chopped fresh sage

4–5 tbsp double cream

salt and pepper

method

1 To make the stuffing, combine the sausagemeat and chestnut purée in a bowl, then stir in the walnuts, apricots and herbs. Stir in enough cream to make a firm, but not dry, mixture and season. Preheat the oven to 220°C/425°F/Gas Mark 7. Fill the neck cavity with the stuffing and close the flap of skin with a skewer.

2 Place the bird in a large roasting tin and rub all over with 40 g/$1^1/2$ oz of the butter. Roast for 1 hour, then lower the oven temperature to 180°C/350°F/Gas Mark 4 and roast for an additional $2^1/2$ hours.

3 Check that the turkey is cooked by inserting the point of a sharp knife into the thigh; if the juices run clear, it is ready. Transfer the bird to a carving board, cover loosely with foil, and let rest.

4 To make the gravy, skim off the fat from the roasting tin then place the pan over a medium heat. Add the red wine and stir with a wooden spoon, scraping up the sediment from the bottom of the pan. Stir in the chicken stock. Mix the cornflour, mustard, vinegar, and 2 teaspoons of water together in a small bowl, then stir into the wine and stock. Bring to the boil, stirring constantly until thickened and smooth. Stir in the remaining butter.

5 Carve the turkey and serve with the stuffing and gravy.

yuletide goose with honey & pears

ingredients

SERVES 4

1 x oven-ready goose,
   weighing 3.5–4.5 kg/7 lb
   12 oz–10 lb
1 tsp salt
4 pears
1 tbsp lemon juice
55 g/2 oz butter
2 tbsp clear honey
seasonal vegetables, to serve

method

1 Preheat the oven to 220°C/425°F/ Gas Mark 7.

2 Rinse the goose and pat dry. Use a fork to prick the skin all over, then rub with the salt. Place the bird upside down on a rack in a roasting tin. Roast in the oven for 30 minutes. Drain off the fat. Turn the bird over and roast for 15 minutes. Drain off the fat. Reduce the temperature to 180°C/350°F/Gas Mark 4 and roast for 15 minutes per 450 g/1 lb. Cover with foil 15 minutes before the end of the cooking time. Check that the bird is cooked by inserting a knife between the legs and body. If the juices run clear, it is cooked. Remove from the oven.

3 Peel and halve the pears and brush with lemon juice. Melt the butter and honey in a saucepan over a low heat, then add the pears. Cook, stirring, for 5–10 minutes until tender. Remove from the heat, arrange the pears around the goose and pour the sweet juices over the bird. Serve with seasonal vegetables.

glazed gammon

ingredients

SERVES 8

1 x 4-kg/9-lb gammon

1 apple, cored and chopped

1 onion, chopped

300 ml/10 fl oz cider

6 black peppercorns

1 bouquet garni

1 bay leaf

about 50 cloves

4 tbsp demerara sugar

method

1 Put the gammon in a large saucepan and add enough cold water to cover. Bring to the boil and skim off the scum that rises to the surface. Reduce the heat and simmer for 30 minutes. Drain the gammon and return to the saucepan. Add the apple, onion, cider, peppercorns, bouquet garni, bay leaf and a few of the cloves. Pour in enough fresh water to cover and bring back to the boil. Cover and simmer for 3 hours 20 minutes.

2 Preheat the oven to 200°C/400°F/Gas Mark 6. Take the saucepan off the heat and set aside to cool slightly. Remove the gammon from the cooking liquid and, while it is still warm, loosen the rind with a sharp knife, then peel it off and discard. Score the fat into diamond shapes and stud with the remaining cloves. Place the gammon on a rack in a roasting tin and sprinkle with the sugar. Roast, basting occasionally with the cooking liquid, for 20 minutes. Serve hot or cold.

festive beef wellington

ingredients

SERVES 4

750 g/1 lb 10 oz thick beef
    fillet
2 tbsp butter
2 tbsp vegetable oil
1 garlic clove, chopped
1 onion, chopped
175 g/6 oz chestnut
    mushrooms
1 tbsp chopped fresh sage
350 g/12 oz frozen puff
    pastry, defrosted
1 egg, beaten
salt and pepper

method

1 Preheat the oven to 220°C/425°F/Gas Mark 7. Put the beef in a roasting tin, spread with butter and season with salt and pepper. Roast for 30 minutes, then remove from the oven. Meanwhile, heat the oil in a pan over a medium heat. Add the garlic and onion and cook, stirring, for 3 minutes. Stir in the mushrooms, sage and salt and pepper to taste and cook for 5 minutes. Remove from the heat.

2 Roll out the pastry into a rectangle large enough to enclose the beef, then place the beef in the middle and spread the mushroom mixture over it. Bring the long sides of the pastry together over the beef and seal with beaten egg. Tuck the short ends over (trim away excess pastry) and seal. Place on a baking sheet, seam-side down. Make 2 slits in the top. Decorate with dough shapes and brush with beaten egg. Bake for 40 minutes. If the pastry browns too quickly, cover with foil. Remove from the oven, cut into thick slices and serve hot.

rack of lamb

ingredients

SERVES 2

1 trimmed rack of lamb,
weighing 250–300 g/
9–10½ oz
1 garlic clove, crushed
150 ml/5 fl oz red wine
1 fresh rosemary sprig,
crushed to release the
flavour
1 tbsp olive oil
150 ml/5 fl oz lamb stock
2 tbsp redcurrant jelly
salt and pepper

for the mint sauce

bunch fresh mint leaves
2 tsp caster sugar
2 tbsp boiling water
2 tbsp white wine vinegar

method

1 Place the rack of lamb in a non-metallic bowl and rub all over with the garlic. Pour over the wine and place the rosemary sprig on top. Cover and leave to marinate in the refrigerator for 3 hours or overnight if possible.

2 Preheat the oven to 220°C/425°F/Gas Mark 7. Remove the lamb from the marinade, reserving the marinade. Pat the meat dry with kitchen paper and season well with salt and pepper. Place it in a small roasting tin, drizzle with the oil and roast for 15–20 minutes, depending on whether you like your meat pink or medium. Remove the lamb from the oven and leave to rest, covered with foil, in a warm place for 5 minutes.

3 Meanwhile, pour the reserved marinade into a small saucepan, bring to the boil over a medium heat and boil rapidly for 5 minutes. Add the stock and redcurrant jelly and simmer, stirring, until the mixture is syrupy.

4 To make the mint sauce, chop the fresh mint leaves and mix together with the sugar in a small bowl. Add the boiling water and stir to dissolve the sugar. Add the white wine vinegar and leave to stand for 30 minutes before serving with the lamb.

5 Carve the lamb into cutlets and serve on warmed plates with the sauce spooned over the top. Serve the mint sauce separately.

herbed salmon with hollandaise sauce

ingredients

SERVES 4

4 salmon fillets, about 175 g/
  6 oz each, skin removed
2 tbsp olive oil
1 tbsp chopped fresh dill
1 tbsp chopped fresh chives,
  plus extra for garnish
salt and pepper

for the hollandaise sauce

3 egg yolks
1 tbsp water
225 g/8 oz butter, cut into
  small cubes
juice of 1 lemon
salt and pepper

to serve

freshly boiled new potatoes
freshly cooked broccoli
sesame seeds, for sprinkling
  (optional)

method

1 Preheat the grill to medium. Rinse the fish fillets under cold running water and pat dry with kitchen paper. Season with salt and pepper. Combine the olive oil with the dill and chives, then brush the mixture over the fish. Transfer to the grill and cook for about 6–8 minutes, turning once and brushing with more oil and herb mixture, until cooked to your taste.

2 Meanwhile, to make the hollandaise sauce, put the egg yolks in a heatproof bowl over a pan of boiling water. Add the water and season with salt and pepper. Lower the heat and simmer, whisking constantly, until the mixture begins to thicken. Whisk in the butter, cube by cube, until the mixture is thick and shiny. Whisk in the lemon juice, then remove from the heat.

3 Remove the fish from the grill and transfer to individual serving plates. Pour over the sauce and garnish with chopped fresh chives. Serve with freshly boiled new potatoes and broccoli, and sprinkle with sesame seeds, if using.

mixed nut roast with cranberry & red wine sauce

ingredients

SERVES 4

2 tbsp butter, plus extra
  for greasing
2 garlic cloves, chopped
1 large onion, chopped
50 g/1³/₄ oz pine kernels,
  toasted
75 g/2³/₄ oz hazelnuts,
  toasted
50 g/1³/₄ oz walnuts, ground
50 g/1³/₄ oz cashew nuts,
  ground
100 g/3¹/₂ oz wholemeal
  breadcrumbs
1 egg, lightly beaten
2 tbsp chopped fresh thyme
250 ml/9 fl oz vegetable stock
salt and pepper
sprigs of fresh thyme,
  to garnish

for the cranberry & red wine sauce

175 g/6 oz fresh cranberries
100 g/3¹/₂ oz caster sugar
300 ml/10 fl oz red wine
1 cinnamon stick

method

1 Preheat the oven to 180°C/350°F/Gas Mark 4. Grease a loaf tin and line it with greaseproof paper. Melt the butter in a saucepan over a medium heat. Add the garlic and onion and cook, stirring, for about 3 minutes. Remove the pan from the heat. Grind the pine kernels and hazelnuts. Stir all the nuts into the pan and add the breadcrumbs, egg, thyme, stock and seasoning.

2 Spoon the mixture into the loaf tin and level the surface. Cook in the centre of the preheated oven for 30 minutes or until cooked through and golden. The loaf is cooked when a skewer inserted into the centre comes out clean. Halfway through the cooking time, make the cranberry and red wine sauce. Put all the ingredients in a saucepan and bring to the boil. Reduce the heat and simmer, stirring occasionally, for 15 minutes.

3 Remove the nut roast from the oven and turn out. Garnish with sprigs of thyme and serve with the cranberry and red wine sauce.

perfect roast potatoes

ingredients

SERVES 6

1.3 kg/3 lb large floury potatoes, such as King Edward, Maris Piper or Desiree, peeled and cut into even-sized chunks

salt

3 tbsp goose fat, duck fat or olive oil

method

1 Preheat the oven to 220ºC/425ºF/ Gas Mark 7.

2 Cook the potatoes in a large saucepan of lightly salted boiling water over a medium heat, covered, for 5–7 minutes. They will still be firm. Remove from the heat. Meanwhile, add the fat to a roasting tin and place in the hot oven.

3 Drain the potatoes well and return them to the saucepan. Cover with the lid and firmly shake the pan so that the surface of the potatoes is slightly roughened to help give a much crisper texture.

4 Remove the roasting tin from the oven and carefully tip the potatoes into the hot fat. Baste them to ensure that they are all coated with it.

5 Roast the potatoes at the top of the oven for 45–50 minutes until they are browned all over and thoroughly crisp. Turn the potatoes and baste again only once during the process or the crunchy edges will be destroyed.

6 Using a slotted spoon, carefully transfer the potatoes from the roasting tin into a warmed serving dish. Sprinkle with a little salt and serve immediately. Any leftovers (although this is most unlikely) are delicious cold.

roasted root vegetables

ingredients

SERVES 4–6

3 parsnips, cut into 5-cm/
  2-inch chunks

4 baby turnips, quartered

3 carrots, cut into 5-cm/
  2-inch chunks

450 g/1 lb butternut squash,
  peeled and cut into
  5-cm/2-inch chunks

450 g/1 lb sweet potatoes,
  peeled and cut into
  5-cm/2-inch chunks

2 garlic cloves, finely chopped

2 tbsp chopped fresh
  rosemary

2 tbsp chopped fresh thyme

2 tsp chopped fresh sage

3 tbsp olive oil

salt and pepper

2 tbsp chopped fresh mixed
  herbs, such as parsley,
  thyme and mint,
  to garnish

method

1 Preheat the oven to 220°C/425°F/Gas Mark 7.

2 Arrange all the vegetables in a single layer in a large roasting tin. Scatter over the garlic and the herbs. Pour over the oil and season well with salt and pepper.

3 Toss all the ingredients together until they are well mixed and coated with the oil (you can leave them to marinate at this stage to allow the flavours to be absorbed).

4 Roast the vegetables at the top of the oven for 50–60 minutes until they are cooked and nicely browned. Turn the vegetables over halfway through the cooking time.

5 Serve with a good handful of fresh herbs scattered on top and a final sprinkling of salt and pepper to taste.

honeyed parsnips

ingredients

SERVES 4

8 parsnips, peeled and
quartered
4 tbsp vegetable oil
1 tbsp honey

method

1 Preheat the oven to 180°C/350°F/Gas Mark 4.

2 Bring a large saucepan of water to the boil. Reduce the heat, add the parsnips and cook for 5 minutes. Drain thoroughly.

3 Pour 2 tablespoons of the oil into a shallow, ovenproof dish and add the parsnips. Mix the remaining oil with the honey and drizzle over the parsnips. Roast in the preheated oven for 45 minutes until golden brown and tender. Remove from the oven and serve.

brussels sprouts with buttered chestnuts

ingredients

SERVES 4

350 g/12 oz Brussels sprouts,
   trimmed

3 tbsp butter

100 g/3^{1}/$_{2}$ oz canned whole
   chestnuts

pinch of nutmeg

salt and pepper

50 g/1^{3}/$_{4}$ oz flaked almonds,
   to garnish

method

1 Bring a large saucepan of water to the boil. Add the Brussels sprouts and cook for 5 minutes. Drain thoroughly.

2 Melt the butter in a large saucepan over a medium heat. Add the Brussels sprouts and cook, stirring, for 3 minutes, then add the chestnuts and nutmeg. Season with salt and pepper and stir well. Cook for another 2 minutes, stirring, then remove from the heat. Transfer to a serving dish, scatter over the almonds and serve.

honey-glazed red cabbage with sultanas

ingredients

SERVES 4

2 tbsp butter

1 garlic clove, chopped

650 g/1 lb 7 oz red cabbage, shredded

150 g/5^1/$_2$ oz sultanas

1 tbsp honey

100 ml/3^1/$_2$ fl oz red wine

100 ml/3^1/$_2$ fl oz water

method

1 Melt the butter in a large saucepan over a medium heat. Add the garlic and cook, stirring, for 1 minute, until slightly softened.

2 Add the cabbage and sultanas, then stir in the honey. Cook for another minute. Pour in the wine and water and bring to the boil. Reduce the heat, cover and simmer, stirring occasionally, for about 45 minutes or until the cabbage is cooked. Serve hot.

christmas pudding

ingredients

SERVES 4

200 g/7 oz currants

200 g/7 oz raisins

200 g/7 oz sultanas

150 ml/5 fl oz sweet sherry

175 g/6 oz butter, plus extra
for greasing

175 g/6 oz brown sugar

4 eggs, beaten

150 g/5^1/$_2$ oz self-raising flour

100 g/3^1/$_2$ oz fresh white or
wholemeal breadcrumbs

50 g/1^3/$_4$ oz blanched
almonds, chopped

juice of 1 orange

grated rind of ^{1}/$_2$ orange

grated rind of ^{1}/$_2$ lemon

^{1}/$_2$ tsp ground mixed spice

holly leaves, to decorate

method

1 Put the currants, raisins and sultanas into a glass bowl and pour over the sherry. Leave to soak for at least 2 hours.

2 Mix the butter and sugar in a bowl. Beat in the eggs, then fold in the flour. Stir in the soaked fruit and sherry with the breadcrumbs, almonds, orange juice and rind, lemon rind and mixed spice. Grease a pudding basin and press the mixture into it, leaving a gap of 2.5 cm/1 inch at the top. Cut a circle of greaseproof paper 3 cm/1^1/4 inches larger than the top of the basin, grease with butter and place over the pudding. Secure with string, then top with 2 layers of foil. Place the pudding in a pan filled with boiling water which reaches two-thirds of the way up the basin. Reduce the heat and simmer for 6 hours, topping up with boiling water when necessary.

3 Remove from the heat and leave to cool. Renew the greaseproof paper and foil and refrigerate for 2–8 weeks. To reheat, steam for 2 hours as before. Decorate with holly and serve.

festive sherry trifle

ingredients

SERVES 8

for the fruit layer

100 g/3^1/$_2$ oz trifle sponges
150 ml/5 fl oz strawberry jam
250 ml/9 fl oz sherry
150 g/5^1/$_2$ oz fresh
    strawberries, hulled
    and sliced
400 g/14 oz canned mixed
    fruit, drained
1 large banana, sliced

for the custard

6 egg yolks
50 g/1^3/$_4$ oz caster sugar
500 ml/18 fl oz milk
1 tsp vanilla essence

for the topping

300 ml/10 fl oz double cream
1–2 tbsp caster sugar
chocolate curls or flakes,
    to decorate

method

1 Spread the trifle sponges with jam, cut them into bite-sized cubes and arrange in the bottom of a large glass serving bowl. Pour over the sherry and leave for 30 minutes.

2 Combine the strawberries, canned fruit and banana and arrange over the sponges. Cover with clingfilm and chill for 30 minutes.

3 To make the custard, put the egg yolks and sugar into a bowl and whisk together. Pour the milk into a pan and warm gently over a low heat. Remove from the heat and gradually stir into the egg mixture, then return the mixture to the pan and stir constantly over a low heat until thickened. Do not boil. Remove from the heat, pour into a bowl and stir in the vanilla. Cool for 1 hour. Spread the custard over the trifle sponge and fruit mixture, cover with clingfilm and chill for 2 hours.

4 To make the topping, whip the cream in a bowl and stir in the sugar to taste. Spread over the trifle, then scatter over the chocolate. Cover with clingfilm and refrigerate for at least 2 hours before serving.

festive mince pies

ingredients

MAKES 12

200 g/7 oz plain flour, plus
    extra for dusting
100 g/3^1/$_2$ oz butter
25 g/1 oz icing sugar
1 egg yolk
2–3 tbsp milk
300 g/10^1/$_2$ oz mincemeat
1 egg, beaten, for sealing and
    glazing
icing sugar, for dusting

method

1 Preheat the oven to 180°C/350°F/Gas Mark 4. Sift the flour into a mixing bowl. Using your fingertips, rub in the butter until the mixture resembles breadcrumbs. Mix in the sugar and egg yolk.

2 Stir in enough milk to make a soft dough, turn out onto a lightly floured work surface and knead lightly until smooth.

3 Shape the dough into a ball and roll out to a thickness of 1 cm/^{1}/$_2$ inch. Use pastry cutters to cut out 12 rounds of 7 cm/2^3/$_4$ inches diameter for the bases and 12 smaller star shapes for the tops. Dust 12 tartlet tins with flour and line with the dough rounds. Prick the bases with a fork, then half-fill each pie with mincemeat. Place the star shapes on top then brush all over with beaten egg. Bake in the preheated oven for 15 minutes. Remove from the oven and cool on a wire rack. Dust with icing sugar and serve.

spiced christmas punch

ingredients

SERVES 10

1 litre/1³/₄ pints of red wine

4 tbsp sugar

1 cinnamon stick

400 ml/14 fl oz boiling water

100 ml/3¹/₂ fl oz brandy

100 ml/3¹/₂ fl oz sherry

100 ml/3¹/₂ fl oz orange
    liqueur, such as Cointreau

2 seedless oranges, cut into
    wedges

2 dessert apples, cored and
    cut into wedges

method

1 Put the wine, sugar and cinnamon into a large saucepan and stir together well. Warm over a low heat, stirring, until just starting to simmer, but do not let it boil. Remove from the heat and strain through a sieve. Discard the cinnamon stick.

2 Return the wine to the pan and stir in the water, brandy, sherry and orange liqueur. Add the orange and apple wedges and warm gently over a very low heat, but do not let it boil. Remove from the heat and pour into a large, heatproof punch bowl. Ladle into heatproof glasses and serve hot.

Granny's
just desserts

Those with a sweet tooth will fondly remember the delicious aromas of puddings and desserts that would emanate from Granny's kitchen. Some are really quick and easy to assemble, whilst others take more time, making them best reserved for special occasions and family get-togethers. Chocolate mousse is always popular and, together with profiteroles, banana splits and Black Forest gateau, will give even the most chocoholic cook enough recipes to indulge in. Pies, strudels and crumbles are included to add fruit to the menu – the fruit can be changed according to taste and season, providing even more diversity.

Along with the traditional favourites, such as baked apples, bread and butter pudding and good old rice pudding, you will find recipes for more exotic – but equally well-loved – desserts like Italian tiramisù, Mississippi mud pie and an American-style baked cheesecake. These are dishes that we've grown up with and adopted as our own, despite their far-flung origins. With such a wide selection you are certainly going to be spoilt for choice when it comes to choosing your Granny's just dessert.

apple pie

ingredients

SERVES 6

for the pastry

350 g/12 oz plain flour

pinch of salt

85 g/3 oz butter or margarine, cut into small pieces

85 g/3 oz lard or white vegetable fat, cut into small pieces

about 6 tbsp cold water

beaten egg or milk, for glazing

for the filling

750 g–1 kg/1 lb 10 oz–2 lb 4 oz cooking apples, peeled, cored and sliced

125 g/4^1/$_2$ oz caster sugar, plus extra for sprinkling

^{1}/$_2$–1 tsp ground cinnamon, mixed spice or ground ginger

1–2 tbsp water (optional)

method

1 To make the pastry, sift the flour and salt into a mixing bowl. Add the butter and lard and rub in with your fingertips until the mixture resembles fine breadcrumbs. Add the water and gather the mixture together into a dough. Wrap the dough and chill in the refrigerator for 30 minutes.

2 Preheat the oven to 220°C/425°F/Gas Mark 7. Roll out almost two-thirds of the pastry thinly and use to line a deep 23-cm/9-inch pie plate or pie tin.

3 Mix the apples with the sugar and spice and pack into the pastry case; the filling can come up above the rim. Add the water if needed, particularly if the apples are not very juicy.

4 Roll out the remaining pastry to form a lid. Dampen the edges of the pie rim with water and position the lid, pressing the edges firmly together. Trim and crimp the edges.

5 Use the trimmings to cut out leaves or other shapes to decorate the top of the pie, dampen and attach. Glaze the top of the pie with beaten egg or milk, make 1–2 slits in the top and place the pie on a baking sheet.

6 Bake in the preheated oven for 20 minutes, then reduce the temperature to 180°C/350°F/ Gas Mark 4 and bake for a further 30 minutes, or until the pastry is a light golden brown. Serve hot or cold, sprinkled with sugar.

latticed cherry pie

ingredients

SERVES 8

for the pastry

140 g/5 oz plain flour,
    plus extra for dusting
1/4 tsp baking powder
1/2 tsp mixed spice
1/2 tsp salt
50 g/1 3/4 oz caster sugar
55 g/2 oz cold unsalted
    butter, diced, plus extra
    for greasing
1 beaten egg, plus extra
    for glazing

for the filling

900 g/2 lb stoned fresh or
    canned cherries, drained
140 g/5 oz granulated sugar
1/2 tsp almond essence
2 tsp cherry brandy
1/4 tsp mixed spice
2 tbsp cornflour
2 tbsp water
25 g/1 oz cold unsalted
    butter, diced
freshly whipped cream or
    ice cream, to serve

method

1 Sift the flour and baking powder. Add the mixed spice, salt and sugar. Rub in the butter until the mixture resembles fine breadcrumbs. Make a well, mix in the beaten egg, then gather to a dough by hand. Divide into two balls, wrap and chill for 30 minutes.

2 Preheat the oven to 220°C/425°F/Gas Mark 7. Roll out the dough into two 30-cm/12-inch circles. Use one to line a 23-cm/9-inch round pie dish.

3 Stir half the cherries and all the sugar over a low heat until the sugar melts. Add the almond essence, cherry brandy and mixed spice. Make a paste with the cornflour and water. Stir into the cherries, turn up the heat and cook until it boils and thickens, stirring constantly. Cool, add the remaining cherries, pour into the pastry case and dot with the butter.

4 Cut the second circle into strips 1-cm/ 1/2-inch wide. Lay strips of pastry evenly across the top of the pie, interweaving them to form a lattice.

5 Trim and crimp the edges. Brush with beaten egg. Cover with foil and bake for 15–20 minutes. Discard the foil, and bake for a further 15 minutes, or until golden. Serve with freshly whipped cream or ice cream.

pear & pecan strudel

ingredients

SERVES 4

2 ripe pears

55 g/2 oz butter

55 g/2 oz fresh white
   breadcrumbs

55 g/2 oz shelled pecan nuts,
   chopped

25 g/1 oz light muscovado
   sugar

finely grated rind of 1 orange

100 g/3^1/$_2$ oz filo pastry,
   thawed if frozen

6 tbsp orange blossom honey

2 tbsp orange juice

sifted icing sugar, for dusting

Greek-style yogurt, to serve
   (optional)

method

1 Preheat the oven to 200°C/400°F/Gas Mark 6. Peel, core and chop the pears. Melt 1 tablespoon of the butter in a frying pan and gently fry the breadcrumbs until golden. Transfer to a bowl and add the pears, nuts, muscovado sugar and orange rind. Put the remaining butter in a small saucepan and heat until melted.

2 Reserve 1 sheet of filo pastry, keeping it well wrapped, and brush the remaining filo sheets with a little melted butter. Spoon some of the nut filling onto the first filo sheet, leaving a 2.5-cm/1-inch margin around the edge. Build up the strudel by placing more buttered filo sheets on top of the first, spreading each one with nut filling as you build up the layers. Drizzle the honey and orange juice over the top.

3 Fold the short ends over the filling, then roll up, starting at a long side. Carefully lift onto a baking sheet, with the join facing up. Brush with any remaining melted butter and crumple the reserved sheet of filo pastry around the strudel. Bake for 25 minutes, or until golden and crisp. Dust with sifted icing sugar and serve warm with Greek-style yogurt, if using.

rhubarb crumble

ingredients

SERVES 6

900 g/2 lb rhubarb
115 g/4 oz caster sugar
grated rind and juice of
    1 orange
cream, yogurt or custard,
    to serve

for the crumble

225 g/8 oz plain or wholemeal
    flour
115 g/4 oz butter
115 g/4 oz soft brown sugar
1 tsp ground ginger

method

1 Preheat the oven to 190°C/375°F/Gas Mark 5.

2 Cut the rhubarb into 2.5-cm/1-inch lengths and place in a 1.7-litre/3-pint ovenproof dish with the sugar and the orange rind and juice.

3 Make the crumble by placing the flour in a mixing bowl and rubbing in the butter until the mixture resembles breadcrumbs. Stir in the sugar and the ginger.

4 Spread the crumble evenly over the fruit and press down lightly using a fork.

5 Bake in the centre of the oven on a baking tray for 25–30 minutes until the crumble is golden brown.

6 Serve warm with cream, yogurt or custard.

lemon meringue pie

ingredients

SERVES 4

for the pastry

150 g/5^{1}/$_{2}$ oz plain flour, plus
   extra for dusting
85 g/3 oz butter, cut into
   small pieces, plus extra for
   greasing
35 g/1^{1}/$_{4}$ oz icing sugar, sifted
finely grated rind of ^{1}/$_{2}$ lemon
^{1}/$_{2}$ egg yolk, beaten
1^{1}/$_{2}$ tbsp milk

for the filling

3 tbsp cornflour
300 ml/10 fl oz water
juice and grated rind of
   2 lemons
175 g/6 oz caster sugar
2 eggs, separated

method

1 To make the pastry, sift the flour into a bowl. Rub in the butter with your fingertips until the mixture resembles fine breadcrumbs. Mix in the remaining ingredients. Knead briefly on a lightly floured work surface. Rest for 30 minutes.

2 Preheat the oven to 180°C/350°F/Gas Mark 4. Grease a 20-cm/8-inch pie dish with butter. Roll out the pastry to a thickness of 5 mm/ 1/4 inch; use it to line the base and sides of the dish. Prick all over with a fork, line with baking paper and fill with baking beans. Bake for 15 minutes. Remove the pastry case from the oven and take out the paper and beans. Reduce the temperature to 150°C/300°F/ Gas Mark 2.

3 To make the filling, mix the cornflour with a little of the water. Put the remaining water in a saucepan. Stir in the lemon juice and rind and cornflour paste. Bring to the boil, stirring.

4 Cook for 2 minutes. Cool a little. Stir in 5 tablespoons of the sugar and the egg yolks and pour into the pastry case.

5 Whisk the egg whites in a clean, grease-free bowl until stiff. Gradually whisk in the remaining sugar and spread over the pie. Bake for a further 40 minutes. Remove from the oven, cool and serve.

mississippi mud pie

ingredients

SERVES 8

for the pastry

225 g/8 oz plain flour, plus
    extra for dusting
2 tbsp cocoa powder
140 g/5 oz butter
2 tbsp caster sugar
1–2 tbsp cold water

for the filling

175 g/6 oz butter
350 g/12 oz soft dark brown
    sugar
4 eggs, lightly beaten
4 tbsp cocoa powder, sifted
150 g/5½ oz plain chocolate
300 ml/10 fl oz single cream
1 tsp chocolate essence
425 ml/15 fl oz whipped
    cream
chocolate flakes and curls,
    to garnish

method

1 To make the pastry, sift the flour and cocoa powder into a mixing bowl. Rub in the butter with your fingertips until the mixture resembles fine breadcrumbs. Stir in the sugar and enough cold water to mix to a soft dough. Wrap the dough and chill in the refrigerator for 15 minutes.

2 Preheat the oven to 190°C/375°F/Gas Mark 5. Roll out the pastry on a lightly floured work surface and use to line a 23-cm/9-inch loose-based flan tin or ceramic flan dish. Line with baking paper and fill with baking beans. Bake in the preheated oven for 15 minutes. Remove the paper and beans from the pastry case and cook for a further 10 minutes until crisp.

3 To make the filling, beat the butter and sugar together in a bowl and gradually beat in the eggs with the cocoa powder. Melt the chocolate and beat it into the mixture with the single cream and the chocolate essence.

4 Reduce the oven temperature to 160°C/325°F/Gas Mark 3. Pour the mixture into the pastry case and bake for 45 minutes, or until the filling has set gently.

5 Let the mud pie cool completely, then transfer to a serving plate. Cover with the whipped cream.

6 Decorate the pie with chocolate flakes and curls and then chill until ready to serve.

bread & butter pudding

ingredients

SERVES 4–6

85 g/3 oz butter, softened
6 slices of thick white bread
55 g/2 oz mixed fruit
  (sultanas, currants and
  raisins)
25 g/1 oz candied peel
3 large eggs
300 ml/10 fl oz milk
150 ml/5 fl oz double cream
55 g/2 oz caster sugar
whole nutmeg, for grating
1 tbsp demerara sugar
cream, to serve

method

1 Preheat the oven to 180°C/350°F/Gas Mark 4.

2 Use a little of the butter to grease a 20 x 25-cm/8 x 10-inch baking dish and butter the slices of bread. Cut the bread into quarters and arrange half overlapping in the dish.

3 Scatter half the fruit and peel over the bread, cover with the remaining bread slices and add the remaining fruit and peel.

4 In a mixing jug, whisk the eggs well and mix in the milk, cream and sugar. Pour this over the pudding and leave to stand for 15 minutes to allow the bread to soak up some of the egg mixture. Tuck in most of the fruit as you don't want it to burn in the oven. Grate the nutmeg over the top of the pudding, according to taste, and sprinkle over the demerara sugar.

5 Place the pudding on a baking tray and bake at the top of the oven for 30–40 minutes until just set and golden brown.

6 Remove from the oven and serve warm with a little pouring cream.

sticky toffee pudding

ingredients

SERVES 4

75 g/2³/4 oz sultanas

150 g/5¹/2 oz stoned dates, chopped

1 tsp bicarbonate of soda

2 tbsp butter, plus extra for greasing

200 g/7 oz brown sugar

2 eggs

200 g/7 oz self-raising flour, sifted

for the sticky toffee sauce

2 tbsp butter

175 ml/6 fl oz double cream

200 g/7 oz brown sugar

zested orange rind, to decorate

freshly whipped cream, to serve

method

1 To make the pudding, put the sultanas, dates and bicarbonate of soda into a heatproof bowl. Cover with boiling water and leave to soak.

2 Preheat the oven to 180°C/350°F/Gas Mark 4. Grease a round cake tin, 20 cm/8 inches in diameter, with butter.

3 Put the remaining butter in a separate bowl, add the sugar and mix well. Beat in the eggs then fold in the flour. Drain the soaked fruits, add to the bowl and mix. Spoon the mixture evenly into the prepared cake tin. Transfer to the preheated oven and bake for 35–40 minutes. The pudding is cooked when a skewer inserted into the centre comes out clean.

4 About 5 minutes before the end of the cooking time, make the sauce. Melt the butter in a saucepan over a medium heat. Stir in the cream and sugar and bring to the boil, stirring constantly. Lower the heat and simmer for 5 minutes.

5 Turn out the pudding onto a serving plate and pour over the sauce. Decorate with zested orange rind and serve with whipped cream.

new york cheesecake

ingredients

SERVES 8–10

sunflower oil, for brushing

85 g/3 oz unsalted butter

200 g/7 oz digestive biscuits, crushed

450 g/1 lb full-fat cream cheese

100 g/3^1/$_2$ oz caster sugar

2 large eggs

1 large egg yolk

100 ml/3^1/$_2$ fl oz soured cream

1^1/$_2$ tsp vanilla essence

blueberry compote, to serve

for the topping

400 ml/14 fl oz soured cream

55 g/2 oz caster sugar

method

1 Preheat the oven to 150°C/300°F/Gas Mark 2. Brush a 20-cm/8-inch springform cake pan with oil. Melt the butter in a saucepan over a low heat. Stir in the digestive biscuits and press evenly into the base of the pan. Bake for 10 minutes, or until lightly browned, then remove and set aside to cool.

2 Place the cream cheese into a large bowl and beat until smooth. Add the sugar and beat for 1 minute. Add the eggs and egg yolk and beat until well combined. Add the soured cream and vanilla essence and stir until smooth. Pour the mixture into the pan and spread evenly.

3 Bake in the oven for 35–45 minutes. Remove from the oven and place on a wire rack (still in the pan). Increase the oven temperature to 200°C/400°F/Gas Mark 6.

4 To make the topping, mix together the cream and sugar, and spread over the top of the cheesecake. Place in the oven and bake for 5–7 minutes. Turn the oven off but leave the cheesecake inside for 1 hour. Remove from the oven and cool in the pan on a wire rack. Cover and refrigerate overnight.

5 Remove the cheesecake from the pan 30 minutes before serving. Spoon the compote on top and chill until ready to serve.

black forest gateau

ingredients

SERVES 8

3 tbsp unsalted butter,
   melted, plus extra for
   greasing
900 g/2 lb fresh cherries,
   stoned and halved
250 g/9 oz caster sugar
100 ml/3^1/$_2$ fl oz cherry
   brandy
100 g/3^1/$_2$ oz plain flour
50 g/1^3/$_4$ oz cocoa powder
^{1}/$_2$ tsp baking powder
4 eggs
1 litre/1^3/$_4$ pints double cream
grated dark chocolate and
   whole fresh cherries,
   to decorate

method

1 Preheat the oven to 180°C/350°F/Gas Mark 4. Grease and line a 23-cm/9-inch springform cake pan. Place the cherries in a saucepan, add 3 tablespoons of the sugar and the cherry brandy and bring to a simmer over medium heat. Simmer for 5 minutes. Drain, reserving the syrup. In a large bowl, sift together the flour, cocoa, and baking powder.

2 Place the eggs in a heatproof bowl and beat in 160 g/5^3/4 oz of the sugar. Place the bowl over a saucepan of simmering water and beat for 6 minutes, or until thickened. Remove from the heat, then gradually fold in the flour mixture and melted butter. Spoon into the cake pan and bake for 40 minutes. Remove from the oven and leave to cool in the pan.

3 Turn out the cake and cut in half horizontally. Mix the double cream and the remaining sugar together and whip lightly until soft peaks form. Spread the reserved syrup over the cut sides of the cake, then spread a layer of whipped cream on the bottom half of the cake, followed by the cherries, and then place the other half on top. Cover the top of the cake with whipped cream, sprinkle over the grated chocolate and decorate with whole fresh cherries.

profiteroles

ingredients

SERVES 4

5 tbsp butter, plus extra
    for greasing
200 ml/7 fl oz cold water
100 g/3$^1/_2$ oz plain flour
3 eggs, beaten

for the cream filling

300 ml/10 fl oz double cream
3 tbsp caster sugar
1 tsp vanilla essence

for the chocolate & brandy sauce

125 g/4$^1/_2$ oz plain dark
    chocolate, broken into
    pieces
2$^1/_2$ tbsp butter
6 tbsp water
2 tbsp brandy

method

1 Preheat the oven to 200°C/400°F/Gas Mark 6.

2 Grease a large baking sheet with butter. To make the pastry, place the water and butter in a saucepan and bring to the boil. Meanwhile, sift the flour into a bowl. Remove the saucepan from the heat and beat in the flour until smooth. Cool for 5 minutes. Beat in enough of the eggs to give the mixture a soft, dropping consistency. Transfer to a piping bag fitted with a 1-cm/$^1/_2$-inch plain nozzle. Pipe small balls onto the baking sheet. Bake for 25 minutes. Remove from the oven. Pierce each ball with a skewer to let steam escape.

3 To make the filling, whip together the cream, sugar and vanilla essence. Cut the pastry balls almost in half, then fill with the cream filling.

4 To make the sauce, gently melt the chocolate and butter with the water in a small saucepan, stirring, until smooth. Stir in the brandy. Pile the profiteroles into individual serving dishes or into a pyramid on a raised cake stand. Pour over the sauce and serve.

chocolate mousse

ingredients

SERVES 4

300 g/10^1/$_2$ oz plain dark
   chocolate

1^1/$_2$ tbsp unsalted butter

1 tbsp brandy

4 eggs, separated

cocoa powder, for dusting

method

1 Break the chocolate into small pieces and place in a heatproof bowl set over a pan of simmering water. Add the butter and melt with the chocolate, stirring, until smooth. Remove from the heat, stir in the brandy and leave to cool slightly. Add the egg yolks and beat until smooth.

2 In a separate bowl, whisk the egg whites until stiff peaks have formed, then fold them into the chocolate mixture. Spoon the mixture into 4 small serving bowls and level the surfaces. Transfer to the refrigerator and chill for at least 4 hours until set.

3 Take the mousse out of the refrigerator, dust with cocoa powder and serve.

traditional tiramisù

ingredients

SERVES 6

20–24 sponge fingers, about
    150 g/5^1/$_2$ oz
2 tbsp cold black coffee
2 tbsp coffee essence
2 tbsp almond liqueur
4 egg yolks
85 g/3 oz caster sugar
a few drops of vanilla essence
grated rind of ^{1}/$_2$ lemon
350 g/12 oz mascarpone
    cheese
2 tsp lemon juice
250 ml/9 fl oz double cream
1 tbsp milk
25 g/1 oz lightly toasted
    flaked almonds
2 tbsp cocoa powder
1 tbsp icing sugar

method

1 Arrange almost half of the sponge fingers in the base of a serving dish. Place the black coffee, coffee essence and almond liqueur in a bowl and mix. Sprinkle just over half of the mixture over the sponge fingers.

2 Place the egg yolks in a heatproof bowl with the sugar, vanilla essence and lemon rind. Stand the bowl over a saucepan of gently simmering water and whisk until very thick and creamy and the whisk leaves a heavy trail when lifted from the bowl.

3 Place the mascarpone cheese in a separate bowl with the lemon juice and beat until smooth. Stir into the egg mixture and, when evenly blended, pour half of the mixture over the sponge fingers and spread out evenly.

4 Add another layer of sponge fingers, sprinkle with the remaining coffee mixture, then cover with the rest of the cheese and egg mixture. Leave to chill in the refrigerator for at least 2 hours, preferably overnight.

5 Whip the cream and milk together until fairly stiff and spread or pipe over the dessert. Sprinkle with the flaked almonds, then sift an even layer of cocoa powder over the top to cover completely. Finally, sift a layer of icing sugar over the cocoa powder and serve.

baked rice pudding

ingredients

SERVES 4–6

1 tbsp melted unsalted butter

115 g/4 oz pudding rice

55 g/2 oz caster sugar

850 ml/1^1/$_2$ pints full-cream milk

^{1}/$_2$ tsp vanilla essence

40 g/1^1/$_2$ oz unsalted butter, chilled and cut into pieces

whole nutmeg, for grating

cream, jam, fresh fruit purée, stewed fruit, honey or ice cream, to serve

method

1 Preheat the oven to 150°C/300°F/Gas Mark 2. Grease a 1.2-litre/2-pint baking dish (a gratin dish is good) with the melted butter, place the rice in the dish and sprinkle with the sugar.

2 Heat the milk in a saucepan until almost boiling, then pour over the rice. Add the vanilla essence and stir well to dissolve the sugar.

3 Cut the butter into small pieces and scatter over the surface of the pudding.

4 Grate the whole nutmeg over the top, using as much as you like to give a good covering.

5 Place the dish on a baking tray and bake in the centre of the oven for 1^1/$_2$–2 hours until the pudding is well browned on the top. You can stir it after the first half hour to disperse the rice.

6 Serve hot topped with cream, jam, fresh fruit purée, stewed fruit, honey or ice cream.

baked apples

ingredients

SERVES 4

25 g/1 oz blanched almonds

55 g/2 oz dried apricots

1 piece stem ginger, drained

1 tbsp clear honey

1 tbsp syrup from the stem
  ginger jar

4 tbsp rolled oats

4 large cooking apples

method

1 Preheat the oven to 180°C/350°F/Gas Mark 4. Using a sharp knife, chop the almonds, apricots and stem ginger very finely. Reserve.

2 Place the honey and syrup in a saucepan and heat until the honey has melted. Stir in the oats and cook gently over a low heat for 2 minutes. Remove the saucepan from the heat and stir in the almonds, apricots and stem ginger.

3 Core the apples, widen the tops slightly and score around the circumference of each to prevent the skins bursting during cooking. Place them in an ovenproof dish and fill the cavities with the stuffing. Pour just enough water into the dish to come about one-third of the way up the apples. Bake in the preheated oven for 40 minutes, or until tender. Serve immediately.

blueberry pancakes

ingredients

MAKES 10–12

140 g/5 oz plain flour

2 tbsp caster sugar

2 tbsp baking powder

$1/2$ tsp salt

225 ml/8 fl oz buttermilk

3 tbsp butter, melted

1 large egg

140 g/5 oz fresh blueberries,
    plus extra to serve

sunflower oil, for oiling

butter and warmed maple
    syrup, to serve

method

1 Preheat the oven to 140°C/275°F/Gas Mark 1. Sieve the flour, sugar, baking powder and salt together into a large bowl and make a well in the centre.

2 Beat the buttermilk, butter and egg together in a separate small bowl, then pour the mixture into the well in the dry ingredients. Beat the dry ingredients into the liquid until a smooth batter is formed. Gently stir in the blueberries.

3 Heat a large frying pan over a medium-high heat until a splash of water dances on the surface. Using a pastry brush, oil the base of the frying pan.

4 Drop about 4 tablespoons of batter separately into the frying pan and spread each out into a 10-cm/4-inch round. Continue adding as many pancakes as will fit in your frying pan. Cook until small bubbles appear on the surface, then flip over with a spatula and cook the other side for a further 1–2 minutes until golden brown.

5 Transfer the pancakes to a warmed plate and place in the preheated oven while you cook the remaining batter, lightly oiling the frying pan as before. Make a stack of the pancakes with baking paper in between each pancake. Serve with a knob of butter on top of each pancake and warm maple syrup for pouring over.

banana splits

ingredients

SERVES 4

4 bananas

6 tbsp chopped mixed nuts,
   to serve

for the vanilla ice cream

300 ml/10 fl oz milk

1 tsp vanilla essence

3 egg yolks

100 g/3^1/$_2$ oz caster sugar

300 ml/10 fl oz double cream,
   whipped

for the chocolate rum sauce

125 g/4^1/$_2$ oz plain chocolate,
   broken into small pieces

2^1/$_2$ tbsp butter

6 tbsp water

1 tbsp rum

method

1 To make the ice cream, heat the milk and vanilla essence in a saucepan until almost boiling. In a bowl, beat together the egg yolks and sugar. Remove the milk from the heat and stir a little into the egg mixture. Transfer the mixture to the pan. Stir over a low heat until thick. Do not boil. Remove from the heat. Cool for 30 minutes, fold in the cream, cover with clingfilm and chill for 1 hour. Transfer into an ice-cream maker and process for 15 minutes. Alternatively, transfer into a freezerproof container and freeze for 1 hour, then place in a bowl and beat to break up the ice crystals. Put back in the container and freeze for 30 minutes. Repeat twice more, freezing for 30 minutes and whisking each time.

2 To make the sauce, melt the chocolate and butter with the water in a saucepan, stirring. Remove from the heat and stir in the rum. Peel the bananas, slice lengthways and arrange on 4 serving dishes. Top with ice cream and nuts and serve with the sauce.

Granny's
baking day

Remember the smells of home-baked cakes, biscuits and scones when you were young? It was on those days that you learned to rub fat into flour with your fingertips to make pastry and to beat sugar and butter together to make cakes. It was fun to sprinkle flour over the kitchen table, roll out biscuit dough and cut it into different shapes – Granny didn't seem to mind the mess.

The best bit was eating the misshapen bits when they were still hot from the oven. This chapter provides recipes for all kinds of delicious goodies – from a classic Victoria sponge cake to indulgent chocolate brownies. Perhaps it will even encourage you to bake with your own children or grandchildren – they will particularly enjoy helping to make the easy nutty flapjacks or assembling the lemon butterfly cakes. All of the recipes in this section are perfect for filling those little gaps in the day, be it mid-morning or tea-time – but make sure you put the rest away in an airtight tin so that there is always something delicious to hand when friends or family come by.

sandwich cake with chocolate topping

ingredients

SERVES 8–10

125 g/4^1/$_2$ oz soft margarine, plus extra for greasing

125 g/4^1/$_2$ oz caster sugar

2 eggs

1 tbsp golden syrup

125 g/4^1/$_2$ oz self-raising flour, sifted

2 tbsp cocoa powder, sifted

for the filling and topping

50 g/1^3/$_4$ oz icing sugar, sifted

25 g/1 oz butter

100 g/3^1/$_2$ oz milk chocolate

a little white chocolate, melted (optional)

method

1 Preheat the oven to 160°C/325°F/Gas Mark 3. Lightly grease two 18-cm/7-inch shallow cake tins.

2 Place all of the ingredients for the cake in a large mixing bowl and beat with a wooden spoon or electric hand whisk to form a smooth mixture.

3 Divide the mixture between the prepared tins and level the tops. Bake in the preheated oven for 20 minutes, or until springy to the touch. Cool for a few minutes in the tins before transferring to a wire rack to cool completely.

4 To make the filling, beat the icing sugar and butter together in a bowl until light and fluffy. Melt the milk chocolate and beat half into the filling mixture. Use the filling to sandwich the 2 cakes together.

5 Spread the remaining melted milk chocolate over the top of the cake. Pipe circles of contrasting melted white chocolate and feather into the milk chocolate with a cocktail stick, if liked. Leave to set before serving.

victoria sponge cake

ingredients

SERVES 8–10

175 g/6 oz butter, at room
  temperature, plus extra
  for greasing
175 g/6 oz caster sugar
3 eggs, beaten
175 g/6 oz self-raising flour
pinch of salt
3 tbsp raspberry jam
1 tbsp caster or icing sugar

method

1 Preheat the oven to 180ºC/350ºF/Gas Mark 4. Grease two 20-cm/8-inch sponge tins and line with greaseproof paper or baking paper.

2 Cream the butter and sugar together in a mixing bowl using a wooden spoon or a hand-held mixer until the mixture is pale in colour and light and fluffy. Add the egg a little at a time, beating well after each addition. Sift the flour and salt and carefully add to the mixture, folding it in with a metal spoon or a spatula.

3 Divide the mixture between the tins and smooth over with the spatula. Place them on the same shelf in the centre of the oven and bake for 25–30 minutes until well risen, golden brown and beginning to shrink from the sides of the tin.

4 Remove from the oven and allow to stand for 1 minute. Loosen the cakes from around the edge of the tins using a palette knife. Turn the cakes out onto a clean tea towel, remove the paper and invert them onto a wire rack (this prevents the wire rack from marking the top of the cakes). When completely cool, sandwich together with the jam and sprinkle with the sugar.

lemon drizzle cake

ingredients

SERVES 8

butter, for greasing

200 g/7 oz plain flour

2 tsp baking powder

200 g/7 oz caster sugar

4 eggs

150 ml/5 fl oz soured cream

grated rind of 1 large lemon

4 tbsp lemon juice

150 ml/5 fl oz sunflower oil

4 tbsp icing sugar

3 tbsp lemon juice

method

1 Preheat the oven to 180°C/350°F/Gas Mark 4. Lightly grease a 20-cm/8-inch loose-bottom round cake tin and line the base with baking paper.

2 Sieve the flour and baking powder into a mixing bowl and stir in the caster sugar.

3 In a separate bowl, whisk the eggs, soured cream, lemon rind, lemon juice and oil together.

4 Pour the egg mixture into the dry ingredients and mix well until evenly combined.

5 Pour the mixture into the prepared tin and bake in the preheated oven for 45–60 minutes until risen and golden brown.

6 Meanwhile, to make the syrup, mix together the icing sugar and lemon juice in a small saucepan. Stir over a low heat until just beginning to bubble and turn syrupy.

7 As soon as the cake comes out of the oven, prick the surface with a fine skewer, then brush the syrup over the top. Leave the cake to cool completely in the tin before turning out and serving.

rich fruit cake

ingredients

SERVES 12

butter, for greasing

175 g/6 oz stoned
  unsweetened dates

125 g/4¹/2 oz ready-to-eat
  dried prunes

200 ml/7 fl oz unsweetened
  orange juice

2 tbsp black treacle

1 tsp finely grated lemon rind

1 tsp finely grated orange rind

225 g/8 oz wholemeal
  self-raising flour

1 tsp mixed spice

125 g/4¹/2 oz seedless raisins

125 g/4¹/2 oz sultanas

125 g/4¹/2 oz currants

125 g/4¹/2 oz dried
  cranberries

3 large eggs, separated

to decorate

1 tbsp apricot jam, warmed

icing sugar, for dusting

175 g/6 oz sugar paste

strips of orange rind

strips of lemon rind

method

1 Grease and line a deep 20-cm/8-inch round cake tin. Chop the dates and prunes and place in a large, heavy-based saucepan. Pour over the orange juice and simmer for 10 minutes. Remove the saucepan from the heat and beat the fruit mixture until puréed. Add the treacle and citrus rinds and leave to cool.

2 Preheat the oven to 160°C/325°F/Gas Mark 3. Sift the flour and mixed spice into a bowl, adding any bran that remains in the sieve. Add the raisins, sultanas, currants and dried cranberries. When the date and prune mixture is cool, whisk in the egg yolks. Whisk the egg whites in a clean bowl until stiff. Spoon the fruit mixture into the dry ingredients and mix together. Gently fold in the egg whites. Transfer to the prepared tin and bake in the preheated oven for 1¹/2 hours. Leave to cool in the tin.

3 Remove the cake from the tin and brush the top with jam. Dust the work surface with icing sugar and roll out the sugar paste thinly. Lay the sugar paste over the top of the cake and trim the edges. Decorate with orange and lemon rind.

classic carrot cake

ingredients

SERVES 12

butter, for greasing

125 g/4^1/$_2$ oz self-raising flour

pinch of salt

1 tsp ground cinnamon

125 g/4^1/$_2$ oz soft brown
 sugar

2 eggs

100 ml/3^1/$_2$ fl oz sunflower oil

125 g/4^1/$_2$ oz carrot, peeled
 and finely grated

25 g/1 oz desiccated coconut

25 g/1 oz walnuts, chopped

50 g/1^3/$_4$ oz butter, softened

50 g/1^3/$_4$ oz soft cheese

225 g/8 oz icing sugar, sifted

1 tsp lemon juice

walnut pieces, to decorate

method

1 Preheat the oven to 180°C/350°F/Gas Mark 4. Lightly grease a 20-cm/8-inch square cake tin and line the base with baking paper.

2 Sift the flour, salt and ground cinnamon into a large bowl and stir in the brown sugar. Add the eggs and oil to the dry ingredients and mix well.

3 Stir in the grated carrot, desiccated coconut and chopped walnuts.

4 Pour the mixture into the prepared tin and bake in the preheated oven for 20–25 minutes, or until just firm to the touch. Leave to cool in the tin.

5 Meanwhile, make the icing. In a bowl, beat together the butter, soft cheese, icing sugar and lemon juice until the mixture is fluffy and creamy.

6 Turn the cake out of the tin and cut into 12 bars or slices. Spread with the icing and then decorate with walnut pieces.

apple streusel cake

ingredients

SERVES 8

115 g/4 oz butter, plus extra
    for greasing
450 g/1 lb cooking apples
175 g/6 oz self-raising flour
1 tsp ground cinnamon
pinch of salt
115 g/4 oz caster sugar
2 eggs
1–2 tbsp milk
icing sugar, for dusting

for the streusel topping

115 g/4 oz self-raising flour
85 g/3 oz butter
85 g/3 oz caster sugar

method

1 Preheat the oven to 180°C/350°F/Gas Mark 4, then grease a 23-cm/9-inch springform cake tin. To make the streusel topping, sift the flour into a bowl and rub in the butter until the mixture resembles coarse crumbs. Stir in the sugar and reserve.

2 Peel, core and thinly slice the apples. To make the cake, sift the flour into a bowl with the cinnamon and salt. Place the butter and sugar in a separate bowl and beat together until light and fluffy. Gradually beat in the eggs, adding a little of the flour mixture with the last addition of egg. Gently fold in half the remaining flour mixture, then fold in the rest with the milk.

3 Spoon the mixture into the prepared tin and smooth the top. Cover with the sliced apples and sprinkle the streusel topping evenly over the top. Bake in the preheated oven for 1 hour, or until browned and firm to the touch. Leave to cool in the tin before opening the sides. Dust the cake with icing sugar before serving.

coffee & walnut cake

ingredients

SERVES 8

for the icing

6 tbsp cocoa powder

2 tbsp cornflour

6 tbsp caster sugar

125 ml/4 fl oz strong black
coffee, cooled

250 ml/9 fl oz milk

walnut halves, to decorate

for the sponge

85 g/3 oz butter, softened,
plus extra for greasing

275 g/9^1/$_2$ oz plain flour

1 tbsp baking powder

85 g/3 oz caster sugar

2 eggs

150 ml/5 fl oz milk

3 tbsp hot strong black coffee

60 g/2^1/$_4$ oz shelled walnuts,
chopped

50 g/1^3/$_4$ oz sultanas

method

1 To make the icing, put all the ingredients into a food processor and process until creamy. Transfer to a saucepan and heat, stirring, over a medium heat until bubbling. Cook for 1 minute, then pour into a heatproof bowl. Leave to cool, then cover with clingfilm and refrigerate for at least 2 hours.

2 Preheat the oven to 190°C/375°F/Gas Mark 5. Grease a 23-cm/9-inch loose-bottomed cake tin with butter and line with baking paper. To make the sponge, sift the flour and baking powder into a bowl, then stir in the sugar. In a separate bowl, beat together the butter, eggs, milk and coffee, then mix into the flour mixture.

3 Stir in the chopped walnuts and the sultanas. Spoon the mixture into the prepared cake tin and level the surface. Transfer to the preheated oven and bake for 1 hour. Remove from the oven and leave to cool. When cool enough to handle, turn out on to a wire rack and leave to cool completely. Spread the icing over the top of the cooled cake, decorate with the walnut halves and serve.

gingerbread

ingredients

MAKES 12-16

450 g/1 lb plain flour
3 tsp baking powder
1 tsp bicarbonate of soda
3 tsp ground ginger
175 g/6 oz unsalted butter
175 g/6 oz soft brown sugar
175 g/6 oz black treacle
175 g/6 oz golden syrup
1 egg, beaten
300 ml/10 fl oz milk
cream or warmed golden
    syrup, to serve

method

1 Line a 23-cm/9-inch square cake tin, 5 cm/ 2 inches deep, with greaseproof or baking paper. Preheat the oven to 160°C/325°F/ Gas Mark 3.

2 Sift the flour, baking powder, bicarbonate of soda and ground ginger into a large mixing bowl. Place the butter, sugar, treacle and syrup in a medium saucepan and heat over a low heat until the butter has melted and the sugar dissolved. Allow to cool a little.

3 Mix the beaten egg with the milk and add to the cooled syrup mixture. Add all the liquid ingredients to the flour mixture and beat well using a wooden spoon until the mixture is smooth and glossy.

4 Pour the mixture into the prepared tin and bake in the centre of the oven for 1^1/2 hours until well risen and just firm to the touch. This gives a lovely sticky gingerbread, but if you like a firmer cake cook for a further 15 minutes.

5 Remove from the oven and allow the cake to cool in the tin. When cool, remove the cake from the tin with the lining paper. Over wrap with foil and place in an airtight tin for up to 1 week to allow the flavours to mature. Cut into wedges and serve cold with tea or coffee or warm with cream and golden syrup.

marbled chocolate & orange teabread

ingredients

SERVES 12

150 g/5¹/₂ oz butter, softened,
   plus extra for greasing
75 g/2³/₄ oz plain chocolate,
   broken into pieces
250 g/9 oz caster sugar
5 large eggs, beaten
150 g/5¹/₂ oz plain flour
2 tsp baking powder
pinch of salt
grated rind of 2 oranges

method

1 Preheat the oven to 180°C/350°F/Gas Mark 4. Grease and line the base and ends of two 450-g/1-lb loaf tins. Place the chocolate in a heatproof bowl set over a saucepan of simmering water, making sure that the base of the bowl does not touch the water. Remove from the heat once the chocolate has melted.

2 Place the butter and sugar in a separate bowl and beat until light and fluffy. Gradually beat in the eggs. Sift the flour, baking powder and salt into the mixture and fold in.

3 Transfer one-third of the mixture to the melted chocolate and stir together. Stir the orange rind into the remaining mixture and place one-quarter of the mixture in each cake tin, spread in an even layer.

4 Drop spoonfuls of the chocolate mixture on top, dividing it between the 2 tins, but do not smooth it out. Divide the remaining orange mixture between the 2 tins, then, using a knife, gently swirl the top 2 layers together to give a marbled effect. Bake in the preheated oven for 35–40 minutes, or until a skewer inserted into the centre comes out clean.

5 Leave to cool in the tins for 10 minutes, then turn out, peel off the lining paper and transfer to a wire rack to cool completely.

banana loaf

ingredients

SERVES 6

unsalted butter, for greasing

125 g/4$^{1}/_{2}$ oz white
    self-raising flour

100 g/3$^{1}/_{2}$ oz light brown self-
    raising flour

150 g/5$^{1}/_{2}$ oz demerara sugar

pinch of salt

$^{1}/_{2}$ tsp ground cinnamon

$^{1}/_{2}$ tsp ground nutmeg

2 large ripe bananas, peeled

175 ml/6 fl oz orange juice

2 eggs, beaten

4 tbsp rapeseed oil

honey, to serve

method

1 Preheat the oven to 180°C/350°F/Gas Mark 4. Lightly grease and line a 450-g/1-lb loaf tin.

2 Sift the flours, sugar, a pinch of salt, and the spices into a large bowl.

3 In a separate bowl, mash the bananas with the orange juice, then stir in the eggs and oil. Pour into the dry ingredients and mix well.

4 Spoon into the prepared loaf tin and bake in the preheated oven for 1 hour, then test to see if it is cooked by inserting a skewer into the centre. If it comes out clean, the loaf is done. If not, bake for a further 10 minutes and test again.

5 Remove from the oven and leave to cool in the tin. Turn the loaf out, slice and serve with honey.

strawberry roulade

ingredients

SERVES 8

3 large eggs
125 g/4¹/₂ oz caster sugar
125 g/4¹/₂ oz plain flour
1 tbsp hot water

for the filling

200 ml/7 fl oz low-fat fromage frais
1 tsp almond essence
225 g/8 oz small strawberries
15 g/¹/₂ oz flaked almonds, toasted
icing sugar, for dusting

method

1 Preheat the oven to 220°C/425°F/Gas Mark 7. Line a 35 x 25-cm/14 x 10-inch Swiss roll tin with baking paper. Place the eggs in a large, heatproof bowl with the caster sugar, place over a saucepan of hot water and, using an electric beater, beat until pale and thick.

2 Remove the bowl from the saucepan. Sift in the flour and fold into the eggs with the hot water. Pour the mixture into the prepared tin and bake in the preheated oven for 8–10 minutes, or until golden and set.

3 Transfer the sponge to a sheet of baking paper. Peel off the lining paper and roll up the sponge tightly along with the baking paper. Wrap in a tea towel and cool until completely cooled.

4 Mix the fromage frais and almond essence together in a bowl. Leave the mixture to chill in the refrigerator until required. Wash, hull and slice the strawberries.

5 Unroll the sponge, spread the fromage frais mixture over the sponge and sprinkle with the sliced strawberries. Roll the sponge up again and transfer to a serving plate. Sprinkle with almonds, lightly dust with icing sugar and serve.

chocolate chip brownies

ingredients

MAKES 12

225 g/8 oz butter, softened,
plus extra for greasing
150 g/5^1/$_2$ oz plain chocolate,
broken into pieces
225 g/8 oz self-raising flour
125 g/4^1/$_2$ oz caster sugar
4 eggs, beaten
75 g/2^3/$_4$ oz pistachio nuts,
chopped
100 g/3^1/$_2$ oz white chocolate,
roughly chopped
icing sugar, for dusting

method

1 Preheat the oven to 180°C/350°F/Gas Mark 4. Grease a 23-cm/9-inch square baking tin and line with baking paper.

2 Place the chocolate and softened butter in a heatproof bowl set over a saucepan of simmering water. Stir until melted, then leave to cool slightly.

3 Sift the flour into a separate bowl and stir in the caster sugar.

4 Stir the beaten eggs into the chocolate mixture, then pour the mixture into the flour and sugar and beat well. Stir in the pistachio nuts and white chocolate, then pour the mixture into the tin, using a palette knife to spread it evenly.

5 Bake in the preheated oven for 30–35 minutes, or until firm to the touch around the edges. Leave to cool in the tin for 20 minutes. Turn out onto a wire rack. Dust with icing sugar and leave to cool completely. Cut into 12 pieces and serve.

nutty flapjacks

ingredients

MAKES 16

115 g/4 oz butter, plus extra
   for greasing
200 g/7 oz rolled oats
115 g/4 oz chopped
   hazelnuts
55 g/2 oz plain flour
2 tbsp golden syrup
85 g/3 oz light muscovado
   sugar

method

1 Preheat the oven to 180°C/350°F/Gas Mark 4, then grease a 23-cm/9-inch square ovenproof dish or cake tin. Place the rolled oats, chopped hazelnuts and flour in a large mixing bowl and stir together.

2 Place the butter, syrup and sugar in a saucepan over a low heat and stir until melted. Pour onto the dry ingredients and mix well. Turn the mixture into the prepared ovenproof dish and smooth the surface with the back of a spoon.

3 Bake in the oven for 20–25 minutes, or until golden and firm to the touch. Mark into 16 pieces and leave to cool in the tin. When completely cooled, cut through with a sharp knife and remove from the tin.

lemon butterfly cakes

ingredients

MAKES 12

115 g/4 oz self-raising flour
$^1/_2$ tsp baking powder
115 g/4 oz butter, softened
115 g/4 oz caster sugar
2 eggs, beaten
finely grated rind of $^1/_2$ lemon
2–4 tbsp milk
icing sugar, for dusting

for the filling

55 g/2 oz butter
115 g/4 oz icing sugar
1 tbsp lemon juice

method

1 Preheat the oven to 190°C/375°F/Gas Mark 5. Place 12 paper cases in a bun tin. Sift the flour and baking powder into a bowl. Add the butter, sugar, eggs, lemon rind and enough milk to give a medium-soft consistency. Beat the mixture thoroughly until smooth, then divide among the paper cases and bake in the preheated oven for 15–20 minutes, or until well risen and golden. Transfer to wire racks to cool.

2 To make the filling, place the butter in a bowl. Sift in the icing sugar and add the lemon juice. Beat well until smooth and creamy. When the cakes are completely cooled, use a sharp-pointed vegetable knife to cut a circle from the top of each cake, then cut each circle in half.

3 Spoon a little buttercream into the centre of each cake and press the 2 semi-circular pieces into it to resemble wings. Dust the cakes with sifted icing sugar before serving.

blueberry muffins

ingredients

MAKES 10–12

250 g/9 oz plain white flour

1 tsp baking powder

pinch of salt

100 g/3¹/₂ oz demerara sugar,
    plus 1 tbsp for sprinkling

1 egg, beaten

225 ml/8 fl oz milk

55 g/2 oz unsalted butter,
    melted

125 g/4¹/₂ oz small fresh
    blueberries

method

1 Preheat the oven to 180°C/350°F/Gas Mark 4.
Line a 12-hole muffin tin with paper cases. Sift
the flour, baking powder and salt into a large
bowl and stir in the sugar.

2 Add the beaten egg, milk and melted butter
to the dry ingredients and stir in lightly until just
combined – do not overmix. Carefully fold in the
blueberries.

3 Spoon the mixture into the paper cases,
taking care not to overfill, and sprinkle with the
remaining sugar.

4 Bake in the preheated oven for 25–30 minutes
until golden brown and firm. Transfer to a wire
rack to cool a little.

scones

ingredients

SERVES 10–12

450 g/1 lb plain flour, plus extra for dusting

$^1/_2$ tsp salt

2 tsp baking powder

55 g/2 oz butter

2 tbsp caster sugar

250 ml/9 fl oz milk

3 tbsp milk, for glazing

strawberry jam and clotted cream, to serve

method

1 Preheat the oven to 220°C/425°F/Gas Mark 7.

2 Sift the flour, salt and baking powder into a bowl. Rub in the butter until the mixture resembles breadcrumbs. Stir in the sugar.

3 Make a well in the centre and pour in the milk. Stir in using a palette knife and make a soft dough.

4 Turn the mixture onto a floured surface and lightly flatten the dough until it is of an even thickness, about 1 cm/$^1/_2$ inch. Don't be heavy-handed, scones need a light touch.

5 Use a 6-cm/2$^1/_2$-inch pastry cutter to cut out the scones and place on the baking tray.

6 Glaze with a little milk and bake for 10–12 minutes, until golden and well risen.

7 Cool on a wire rack and serve freshly baked with strawberry jam and clotted cream.

shortbread

ingredients

MAKES 8

115 g/4 oz butter, cut into small pieces, plus extra for greasing

175 g/6 oz plain flour, plus extra for dusting

pinch of salt

55 g/2 oz caster sugar, plus extra for dusting

method

1 Preheat the oven to 150°C/300°F/Gas Mark 2.

2 Grease a 20-cm/8-inch fluted cake tin or flan tin.

3 Mix together the flour, salt and sugar. Rub the butter into the dry ingredients. Continue to work the mixture until it forms a soft dough. Make sure you do not overwork the shortbread or it will be tough, not crumbly as it should be.

4 Lightly press the dough into the cake tin. If you don't have a fluted tin, roll out the dough on a lightly floured board, place on a baking tray and pinch the edges to form a scalloped pattern.

5 Mark into 8 pieces with a knife. Prick all over with a fork and bake in the centre of the oven for 45–50 minutes until the shortbread is firm and just coloured.

6 Allow to cool in the tin and dust with the sugar. Cut into portions and remove to a wire rack. Store in an airtight container in a cool place until needed.

chocolate chip cookies

ingredients

MAKES 18

125 g/4^1/$_2$ oz soft margarine,
   plus extra for greasing
175 g/6 oz plain flour
1 tsp baking powder
85 g/3 oz light muscovado
   sugar
5 tbsp caster sugar
^{1}/$_2$ tsp vanilla essence
1 egg
125 g/4^1/$_2$ oz dark chocolate
   chips

method

1 Preheat the oven to 190°C/375°F/Gas Mark 5. Lightly grease two baking trays.

2 Place all of the ingredients in a large mixing bowl and beat until well combined.

3 Place tablespoonfuls of the mixture onto the baking trays, spacing them well apart to allow for spreading during cooking.

4 Bake in the preheated oven for 10–12 minutes or until the cookies are golden brown.

5 Using a palette knife, transfer the cookies to a wire rack to cool completely before serving.

classic oatmeal cookies

ingredients

MAKES 30

175 g/6 oz butter or
   margarine, plus extra
   for greasing
275 g/9^1/$_2$ oz demerara sugar
1 egg
4 tbsp water
1 tsp vanilla essence
375 g/13 oz rolled oats
140 g/5 oz plain flour
1 tsp salt
^{1}/$_2$ tsp bicarbonate of soda

method

1 Preheat the oven to 350°F/180°C/Gas Mark 4 and grease a large baking sheet.

2 Cream the butter and sugar together in a large mixing bowl. Beat in the egg, water and vanilla essence until the mixture is smooth.

3 In a separate bowl, mix the oats, flour, salt and bicarbonate of soda. Gradually stir the oat mixture into the butter mixture until thoroughly combined.

4 Put 30 rounded tablespoonfuls of cookie mixture onto the greased baking sheet, making sure they are well spaced. Transfer to the preheated oven and bake for 15 minutes, or until the cookies are golden brown.

5 Remove the cookies from the oven and place on a wire rack to cool before serving.

white bread

ingredients

MAKES 1 LOAF

450 g/1 lb strong white flour,
plus 2 tbsp for dusting

1 tsp salt

7 g/¼ oz easy-blend dried
yeast

1 tbsp vegetable oil or melted
butter, plus 1 tsp for
greasing

300 ml/10 fl oz warm water

method

1 Mix the flour, salt and yeast together in a mixing bowl. Add the oil and water and stir well to form a soft dough.

2 Turn the dough out onto a lightly floured board and knead well by hand for 5–7 minutes. Alternatively, use a free-standing electric mixer for this and knead the dough with the dough hook for 4–5 minutes. The dough should have a smooth appearance and feel elastic.

3 Return the dough to the bowl, cover with clingfilm and leave to rise in a warm place for 1 hour. When it has doubled in size, turn it out onto a floured board and knead again for 30 seconds; this is known as 'knocking back'. Knead it until smooth.

4 Shape the dough into a rectangle the length of the tin and three times the width. Grease the tin well, fold the dough into three lengthways and put it in the tin with the join underneath for a well-shaped loaf. Cover and leave to rise in a warm place for 30 minutes until it has risen well above the tin.

5 Preheat the oven to 220°C/425°F/Gas Mark 7. Bake in the centre of the preheated oven for 25–30 minutes until firm and golden brown. Test that the loaf is cooked by tapping it on the bottom – it should sound hollow. Cool on a cooling rack for 30 minutes. Store in an airtight container in a cool place for 3–4 days.